Josh!

Enjoy ..

MW01119898

Gold Digger Nation

Why you should remain single.

Hal Roback

CONTENTS

READ THIS!

The most important decision you'll ever make in your life is whether to marry and, if so, whom you will marry. I'm addressing this book to men and, yes, women too, who are contemplating entering the institution of matrimony. I want this book to inform you about what lies ahead. There is good reason to be nervous, anxious, and scared—not for all of you, but most probably half of you! I'm going to explain why you should be wary, and I will also raise some important questions regarding the whole concept of marriage.

If you live in the U.S., Canada, Great Britain, or Australia, to name a few, you're living in a Gold Digger Nation. The impact of this could be the biggest obstacle you'll ever face with a lifetime of consequences. I want to inform you about what might possibly happen—and not just like a 5 percent chance, but more like an 80 percent predictability. Most people who experience the aftereffects of our Gold Digger Nation wish that they had known what they were getting into. It is for this reason I've written *Gold Digger Nation*.

I never thought I would ever write a book. You see, I'm not a professional writer. I don't have the typical background of someone who writes books on subjects like this. I'm not a lawyer, psychologist, or a professor with the type of credentials that people perk up and listen to. I'm just a dupe who has been a casualty of our Gold Digger Laws living in a Gold Digger Nation.

I've never protested for any cause, written a letter to the editor, or called a radio talk show to vent or express my opinion on any subject. Yet I felt compelled to communicate the following as you just aren't aware of what lies ahead when you walk down the aisle.

No one has written a book specifically on this subject. I'm actually surprised and would have been delighted if I had found the message out there as it would have excused me from this task, which didn't come easily to me. There are a plethora of books on the subject of marriage, family law, and divorce, and there are many that deal specifically with the topic of child custody. In this book, I'm going to focus on the dollars and cents of marriage and divorce and the impact of living in a Gold Digger Nation.

I can hear the sarcasm now: "Who cares about a bunch of millionaires being ripped off through the divorce process? Don't we have bigger problems to deal with?" The answer is no, we don't have bigger problems to deal with. This is huge, and it has ramifications in all kinds of related areas. If we're exposed to a legal system that refuses to dish out justice, then we're dealing with a court that is unjust. I would say that's a big problem. If we are dealing with procedures and practices that run contrary to our morals and values as a society, then we are heading down a slippery slope. If I didn't believe that this specific issue could very well be the "tipping point" for either the demise or the rejuvenation of our Western world, I would have not written this book. Yes, living in our Gold Digger Nation is that important an issue, and it is one which will have horrible ripple effects.

When we have a system in place that allows an individual to profit from divorce, and so chooses it over marriage, then we have an erosion of that institution and our morals and values for allowing this. It not only encourages divorce, but it affects marriage right from the get go. Marriage today is not your mother and father's marriage. Gold Digger Laws have turned this institution on its head, and it's getting worse, not better. Many men and, yes, women too, who have found out the realities of our family laws are just saying *no* to marriage. More and more are abstaining from this institution where "heads she wins, and tails you lose." These are the enlightened ones. They're making an informed choice. My objective is to give you the information for you to make yours.

Only a small minority of people have any idea what lurks around the corner on the road to matrimony. If they did, there would be fewer marriages. The pendulum has been hijacked by special interests and moved all the way to the extreme. How we got there and who is behind it will be discussed in this book. What's more important is what this means to you personally—not only in divorce court, but in your marriage as well if you so choose. Yes, our Gold Digger Nation affects your marriage right from the start.

My objective in communicating this information is to start pushing the pendulum back to where it belongs. This won't be easy as there are very powerful and influential groups with vested interests in keeping the pendulum set exactly where it is—at your expense, of course.

I'm going to shock you with the realities of our Gold Digger Nation. Your logical reaction will most probably be, "This won't happen to *me*. This happens to people who break their marriage vows, who aren't good husbands or fathers." Not too many people tie the knot thinking it's going to happen to them. You see, this Gold Digger Nation is still such a well-kept secret that you're not supposed to know about it until it's an afterthought, and then it's too late. Is my objective to scare you? To be honest, yes. But I'll settle for informing you and letting you decide what you're going to do.

There are two parts to this book. The first part is the story of a pretty typical scenario of a modern marriage/ cohabitation in our Gold Digger Nation. It's important to tell this story because what happened in this case has absolutely no bearing in family law courts. This story will have an immense effect on you even though the court couldn't care less, and this is why it has to be told.

In the second part, we canvass the important details of our Gold Digger Nation—things you'll want to know before saying "I do." Here we will discuss how this all came about, the procedures and processes of our divorce industry, the bundle of entitlements that our courts dish out at your expense, and finally some suggestions to set the pendulum back to its rightful location. I've also included a section addressed to my son and daughter, and it's for you and yours as well.

In this book I've used the masculine gender to represent the "dupe" and the female gender for the awards recipient, but I want you to know that there are female dupes and male award recipients as well.

I have many people to thank for helping me with this undertaking. First and foremost, to my sister, Karen, the artist, for creating the cover and the other fifty illustrations that we didn't use. To my talented nephew, Jarrad, who helped with Photoshop and with research as well. To my editor, Sandy, who is a saint for putting up with a rookie like me who had never written before and was invaluable in educating me and getting this project to completion. I would like to thank Marly and Jessica for their advice and professionalism and for proofreading and editing the book To my book publisher, Book Surge, and especially Shauna for her patience. To Tim and the team at Ontrack Communications for their creative website design. Lastly, to my family and friends who encouraged, advised, and provided ideas.

I hope that you will visit the Web site, www.gold-diggernation.com, and get involved in your own way to change the status quo. Whether it be spreading the word, recommending the book, or coming to one of my lectures, I hope you'll pass on what you've learned in this book and educate others about our Gold Digger Nation.

GOLD DIGGER NATION:
PART ONE

Section I: The Dupe

CHAPTER ONE

At least once a week for the past eleven years, my best friend, Dave Salzman, and I have met at one of Manhattan's numerous watering holes after work. For me it's not really after work—it's more like halftime. I'm in the restaurant business, and happy hour represents a segue between lunch and dinner business.

This particular Thursday afternoon, we met at Bloody Mary's, an institution of a saloon, located at Second Avenue and Fifty-seventh. It's a holdout from the fifties when it was frequented by various bon vivants, B-list celebs, and wannabes. These days, it's full of the financial and professional crowd, up-and-comers, and those who want to be associated with them—all these "silver bullets," trying to launch into the next stratosphere of money and position and to live out their dreams. After all, this is New York—not a place for the faint of heart, the meek, or the passive.

It was 5:40 when Dave entered the bar looking for me. I waved to him from the booth I'd secured as I'd already ordered a beverage. I watched as he made his way through the packed, happy hour crowd that was standing three-deep at the bar. Dave stopped to chat with a girl he knew sitting at a booth on the other side of the room. She was with two of her girlfriends. I could see that Dave greeted the other two to whom he had just been introduced. After a short conversation, I watched them keep an eye on him as he walked through the bar, waving to the bartender on his way to join me.

"Hey, Bobby, really packed in here tonight. You must be glad to see this." Dave knew that I specifically chose Bloody Mary's as I wanted to check out the competition for my newest restaurant opening nearby in four weeks.

"I love seeing this place so busy. This is my market, and it's got a good clientele. It's just hard for me to relax in this setting. You know me—I can't relax in restaurants or bars."

"Bobby, just chill, you're always so uptight. It's not your place—what do you care? Trish, baby, a vodka martini for me and another Diet Coke for the young lad. Thanks, doll." Trish giggled as she left.

Dave has always been an extrovert, the life of the party, ever since I first met him at university twenty-one years ago. Now, he's a very successful mortgage broker, which suits his personality and style perfectly. He loves to have a good time and is comfortable with people. Folks have always been drawn to him, both women and men. I think he would be successful at anything he put his mind to, but he loves what a mortgage broker's life brings him. Dave can work anywhere—at home, on his boat, wherever he can get cell phone reception. He hates the constraints of an office and all the associated trimmings like a tie, office protocol, and corporate games. He just wants to live life to its fullest and make a damn good living arranging mortgages for hundreds of people he could meet, network with, and be referred to. We never talked about how much we made, but I think Dave was pulling in a seven-figure income.

In college, Dave was quite the ladies' man, and his present-day bachelor status reconfirms his continued mind-set and lifestyle. I think this was a big part of the attraction to him. I know it was for me. Dave is my polar opposite in many ways. I'm an introvert, serious, a detailed workaholic, and truth be known, very scared of financial ruin. I lost my dad at an early age and watched as my mother worked long hours with not much to show for her hard work. We grew up in Cleveland; my dad was a technician at the B. F. Goodrich aviation division. He had a massive heart attack at forty-nine and never made it to the hospital. Growing up without him and with responsibilities to help put food on the table makes a fourteen-year-old grow up real fast. I guess I looked up to Dave for all that I wasn't.

"Hey, who were those girls you spoke to on your way in?"

"Oh yeah, Nicole…I met her at a networking function a month or two ago. Did you see the blonde with her? Mucho gorgeous! Let's go over; I'll introduce you to them."

At this time, our drinks arrived.

"Not now—in a while."

"Come on, Bobby, you got to get back in the saddle. It's been two years since your divorce. Let's go; I'll introduce you."

Without a pause, Dave was up and walking towards Nicole and her friends, assuming I was right behind him. When he got there, he gave an aggressive wave with silent instructions to come over. Embarrassed, I went over and joined him.

"Nicole, Katie, and Lisa, I want you to meet the infamous restaurateur, Bobby Lakeland. Bobby is opening his newest restaurant not too far from here in around a month, Aqua Blue."

"Wow, that's so exciting," said Nicole. "You should hire my friend Lisa; she's a fantastic waitress."

This made Lisa a little embarrassed, and she gestured to Nicole to stop.

I made eye contact with Lisa, and I couldn't help but notice that the color of her eyes was pretty close to aqua blue. There was no question that she was a very attractive girl—a head turner would be a good description. She appeared to be in her midtwenties, fashion conscious with a model's frame, and natural-blonde hair. She was gifted with good looks, not disguised behind a ton of makeup and styling gel like Nicole. Her other friend, Katie, was a wholesome plain Jane and looked like a blank canvas sitting next to Lisa.

Looking directly at Lisa, I handed her my card and quickly scribbled the Aqua Blue manager's name and cell phone number on the back.

"We're looking for qualified, experienced professionals for Aqua Blue. Please give the manager a call if you have any interest in making a change. I'm sure he would be pleased to talk to you about joining our team."

I watched as Lisa took the card and studied all the information on it. She smiled at me with those gorgeous blue eyes and said, "Thanks, I just might take you up on it."

I was nervous and uncomfortable at this point, so I quickly added, "It was very nice meeting all of you. Dave, I have to run; I'll call you." Then I exited Bloody Mary's onto Second Avenue.

CHAPTER TWO

A few days after that chance meeting, I stopped by the almost-completed Aqua Blue. My vision was coming together—a traditional steakhouse with elegant components. The restaurant business had been going through a metamorphosis. My sector, the casual dinner house level, was really changing, and Aqua Blue was my attempt to meet the psychographic shifts of a very trendy market that was craving the combination of established cuisine in a new-age environment. The economy was robust; the city was now vibrant after Mayor Giuliani had cleaned it up. Aqua Blue was to be the eclectic yet traditional steak house with panache and modern style—kind of like comfy jeans but with a designer shirt and a thousand-dollar blazer. So much of the success of the concept was based on intangibles, but if this was an easy task, everyone could do it and be successful. In reality, only a few have the ability to put these visionary components together.

The bar was the first thing the customer saw. It was red mahogany and designed in a kidney shape with the bartenders in the circle. I had recruited the two evening bartenders myself, a man and a woman with a lot of experience. The woman had come from the Saratoga polo clubhouse and reeked of good taste. She would set the tone just right.

It was this sort of attention to detail that had made my restaurants successful. I fussed over everything from construction to the serving plates. In the beginning of the business, I recruited my chefs by visiting the Culinary Institute in Hyde Park and talking to their instructors about who showed talent and the Calvinistic work ethic necessary to make it in a high-end Manhattan restaurant. When I found budding chefs, I gave them their start, much like the art representatives who were raiding the fine arts master's programs around the city to find new artists to represent. In fact, one of my chefs was the first to get his own show when the Food Network came about.

This strategy still works. Today I have restaurants in Manhattan, Duchess County, Connecticut, and Saddle Ridge, New Jersey, and they are on every list that matters—from *Zagat's* to the *New Yorker*. Every once in a while, I receive an inquiry to locate outside of the New York area from a developer who has patronized one of my restaurants or someone who has heard or read about one of them. Although it sounds tempting and is always flattering, I feel most comfortable having restaurants within driving distance.

I found Hy Prescott, short for Hyland, the restaurant's manager, standing amidst the construction in the nearly completed kitchen and talking with one of the construction crew just as Lisa stepped into the restaurant. I was really excited to see her and felt my heart beat a little faster. It was ten o'clock. I noticed her immediately because of the way she was dressed. She was wearing a stark black wraparound dress over a starched, white, cotton blouse with long, cuffed sleeves. With her blonde hair in a chignon, Lisa looked like a 1940s movie starlet. Seeing her dressed like that displayed her poise and charisma. She was elegant, like Gwyneth Paltrow or Kim Basinger. Seeing her for the first time standing up, she appeared to be approximately five foot six inches and around 115 pounds and looked like a perfect size four.

I didn't want to get into Hy's business, so I stepped into his office out of view, but I have to confess I eavesdropped on the interview. I remember a little of it, and in retrospect her answers were so Lisa—manipulated to say exactly what Hy would want to hear.

She introduced herself, and I learned that her full name was Lisa Babcock. Hy went through the basics with her—what she was making, how many tables she served, and how much she got in tips. Then Hy asked her the bottom-line question: "Why would you quit?"

She didn't hesitate. "A few reasons. I checked Mr. Lakeland's business out on the Internet. Lakeland Restaurants looks like the kind of corporation I would like to work in. I appreciate your mission. Also, I feel like I need a change."

Hy told her he would get back to her and that training was starting the following week. Knowing Hy, this told me he was going to hire her after he asked for her references. I moved out of the office, stepping around the team hanging valances on the bay windows overlooking Sixty-fifth Street. It was impulsive—that's all

I can say. I don't know why I didn't just stay in the office. Obviously, there was some chemistry, even then. "Hi, nice to see you again. I'm glad you took me up on my suggestion. Have you met the manager yet?"

"Yes, I met him, and we just finished the interview. Aqua Blue looks great; I hope my references work out and he calls me back for training."

We shook hands, and I watched as she left the restaurant onto Second Avenue.

The night of the Aqua Blue pre-opening party, June 30, was a perfect New York early summer evening, breezy with temperatures in the seventies. The restaurant was awash with flowers, some good luck arrangements from suppliers and friends, which the designer had relegated to the front of the restaurant on the floor in front of the Second Avenue window. The rest of the room was adorned with huge, glorious arrangements—some wildflowers and arrangements of precious orchids. All shades of lavender marked another arrangement. Guests were served tapas and drinks. The restaurant was packed.

Lisa stood at the front of the room at the hostess desk. Her black top with lace trim and size-four skirt fit perfectly. It had been an easy call to upgrade her to hostess. The restaurant business is so intricate. The image projected by whomever you have greeting and seating guests is very important in setting the right tone and image for your concept. She was gorgeous and had the right style. That was the image we wanted to project when customers first entered the restaurant. When she showed up for the training, Hy offered her a salary that was large enough to cover what she would have been making as a waitress, including what tips would have brought in. She was delighted. And that was that. The job was easier than waitressing.

It is common practice for a restaurant of Aqua Blue's level to have a few pre-opening parties. For one reason, they serve as rehearsals prior to opening for the paying public by working out any kinks, and secondly, to prime the pump by inviting various movers and shakers to start to create the buzz. So much of a restaurant is smoke and mirrors, perception, and creating word-of-mouth chattering through the marketplace. I always invited key executives in the area, government officials, and synergistic business professionals such as hotel concierges, hair salon owners, and theatre managers, to name a few.

When Dave Salzman arrived, Lisa gave him a special hello and complimented his date on her dress. She made certain she was the hostess leading them to one of the four balcony tables. Lisa made small talk with Dave about the success of the evening and then called their server over to the table, wishing them a terrific meal. I took notice of her handling my special guest with élan.

Midway through the evening, as usual, I checked on how things were going and how many more invited guests were still to arrive.

"Everything is under control, Mr. Lakeland," one of the other hostesses said.

"Please call me Bobby. Mr. Lakeland was my father's name." This always got a laugh.

Lisa was standing in front of the podium and watching the exchange. My smile was still in place.

"I do have something I would like to talk to you about." The other two hostesses' heads turned towards her as though choreographed, in unison.

"Is something wrong?"

"No, but I'd like to make an appointment with you."

"Of course." I suggested we meet on Friday since I was granting myself Thursday off to go sailing.

"You are working evenings, right?" I asked.

"Yes."

"How about if we meet before your shift on Friday?"

"That's fine," Lisa replied.

The two other hostesses, Barbara and Jean, went off to the ladies' room together. Already Lisa had made enemies of her coworkers, but I was to learn she was used to it. Nicole and Katie were the only two women she had ever befriended, and that was because the three of them balanced each other out. But Lisa didn't care.

Thursday found me sailing in the Long Island Sound. When Dave Salzman bought his weekend home, he did not bother with the Hamptons or the mountains of upstate New York. His idea of paradise was sailing and windsurfing, so he bought a house near Dix Hills that overlooked the sound. On a clear day, out of Dave's living room window he could see straight through to Connecticut.

In truth, I was no sailor. There was nothing in my upbringing to prepare me for the intricacies with which Dave mastered the twenty-three-foot Jeanneau, but Dave taught me to steer. So our days together on the sound worked out fine so long as there was adequate wind.

It was one of those July days when everything is aligned for good sailing. Dave and I had been discussing a real estate investment and mortgage package he was working on in Costa Rica.

"What a beautiful place, Bobby. We have to take a trip down there." We clicked our cans of beer together. Dave maneuvered the boat to stay quiet while we reflected. Our friendship was built upon history but also the differences between us.

"Did I tell you about that woman I met on Fire Island?"

I shrugged. I was used to Dave's relentless need to regurgitate his sexual adventures. So he told me about the lawyer he had met who was handling high-profile criminal cases for Gideon Sachs, including an imam incarcerated as a presumed international terrorist.

Then we had the conversation we had been having for ages and that always ended up the same way.

"So what are you waiting for?" Dave would say, or something like it.

"I don't want to date. I just can't handle the process."

"Bobby, it's been years since you and Barbara separated. How long are you going to isolate? You don't have to get serious, just enough to connect sexually. How about the new hostess at Aqua Blue? She's hot!"

I looked at Dave and smiled and said, "I've got two words for you: sexual harassment."

"That woman doesn't look like the sexual harassment type." I remember him saying this.

"What are you talking about? Women sue for harassment all the time," I said.

Dave replied, "She's into partying. Look at her next time you see her. She's open."

The conversation went on in this direction for a while and drifted off.

The sun lulled us into a reflective mode. I mulled over Dave's advice about dating. But I wasn't Dave. I wasn't cool and detached. I craved intimacy, but I was just recovering from a bad marriage and a bitter divorce trial. I was also in the process of healing my relationship with a seven-year-old son who had been the victim of a custody battle. I had been scorched. The last thing I needed was another relationship in my life. I was better off keeping my mind on business.

The head office of Lakeland Restaurants consisted of our accounting and personnel departments, my administrative assistant, a former restaurant manager who was in a debilitating car accident and couldn't handle the restaurant grind any longer, and my longtime, trusted comptroller, who looked after major purchasing contracts, insurance, and landlord relations and oversaw the accounting department. Ricky Wong had been with me for close to twenty years. He had been a busboy at my first restaurant and went to night school to learn bookkeeping while he worked days at the restaurant. I trusted him with the tremendous responsibility and cherished our close relationship.

My office was full of memorabilia, with lots of photos of restaurant patrons, staff functions, and restaurant concept renderings. It was very humble and eclectic, not anyone's idea of a slick corporate package.

On Friday, Lisa showed up at the corporate office of Lakeland Restaurants, located on Park and Thirty-fourth. She wasn't wearing her hostess uniform. Instead, she was carrying it in a garment bag and was dressed in a navy silk sheath held up by straps and with fuchsia stripes down the sides. She wore a large, garnet cocktail ring. Her shoes were the same fuchsia as the dress, high-heeled sandals. I remember her outfit quite clearly. Everything about her said upscale. She was carrying a sketchpad. When I saw her at my office door, I waved her in and motioned for her to take a seat. I brought my phone call to an end.

To be honest, my heart was racing as I attempted to hide my schoolboy attraction to her. I greeted her professionally and added, "Nice to see you out of uniform."

She looked at me, not smiling. I admired her direct look. I attributed this to honesty and openness.

"Well, actually, the uniforms are what I would like to talk to you about." In a no-nonsense way, she opened the sketchpad. She had drawn a blue sheath, very similar to what she was wearing but with cap sleeves, though the sketch indicated the dress would be made of rayon.

"All of the women would be able to wear this—the thin ones and…"

"The larger girls," I prompted.

"Right. They would look good in a sheath. You don't want it to be aqua because that's a little coy, but, well, you know, peacock blue is the new black!"

We shared a smile.

"I will look into it, Lisa, and I think it's great that you put so much time into this. Are you attending Pratt or FIT?"

"No, I just like fashion. I have no formal education." She looked at her watch. Then she fired away with probing questions. Perhaps I should have noted that they sounded like something she might have read in *The Rules* or *Cosmopolitan Magazine* about "How to Make Him Pay Attention When You Only Have Five Minutes."

She said, "What about you? How does someone get to be a big-time restaurant owner? Obviously you are way more talented than most of the people opening restaurants in town."

So I gave her the high points. During high school, I worked in restaurants and enjoyed the atmosphere and witnessing the happy events in people's lives. After high school, I went to cooking and baking school, and after working for a few years, I went back and got my degree in hotel and restaurant administration. I noticed that Lisa's blue eyes were directly on me, and to be honest, it felt good to open up.

"When was this?" she asked.

I replied, "In the early seventies."

"How did you get to own restaurants?"

"How much time do you have before your shift starts?"

I suggested we hop in a cab and I'd finish the story en route. I told her about the small, college town diner I bought in New Paltz, NY, how I renovated and changed the concept. I doubled sales and was able to sell it for enough to get me going in Manhattan. From there, I opened my second location, and the rest is history, as they say.

She continued her questions. "Why did you move to the city?"

"My wife wanted to live here."

"Do you have children?"

"I have a son. He's seven. But my wife and I are divorced." The more I used those words, the easier it got, though Lisa was the first "available" woman I had told, and I wasn't sure why the words tumbled out so easily.

"I'm sorry. How long were you married?"

"Almost five years. But enough about me. And what about you? You're twenty-three?"

"Very good," she said in astonishment. "Well, I've never been married." She waited for a response and didn't get one. "I'd like a family, but first I need a boyfriend, don't you think?"

We shared a laugh, but I couldn't help but think there was a method to her questions and statements. Was she sending me a clear communication?

I was thinking the conversation had turned awfully personal in a very short time. I was a private man, nearly secretive. But I had gone to a therapist when my marriage fell apart and was learning to express myself with less reservation. Besides, there was something about this young woman that encouraged me to open up.

"What do you do when you're not working?" she asked.

"Yesterday I went sailing with Dave, my best friend. Remember? You met him at Bloody Mary's."

"He was at the opening."

"That's right," I replied.

"Do you fish? I love to fish, and the trout fishing is fabulous upstate."

"Can't say I fish."

She said, "Well, an intense man like yourself should get away once in a while with a fly-fishing pole…"

"That's interesting advice," I answered.

"I have to say, I looked at your site and peeked inside your other restaurants."

I was caught off guard by this.

"You have quite an individual style. All your restaurants are different, but they all have a defined feel to them. I guess that's why they're all successful."

"What made you check my site?" I asked.

"I was taking a job in your restaurant. I wanted to know more about your business, about the company, and you, of course!"

"Well, you are quite a conscientious employee, and I'm glad you've joined our company." I pointed to the sketch in front of me. "I'm going to take this sketch and see what Hy can do about the uniforms."

The cab pulled up to Aqua Blue, and we parted company. Lisa said over her shoulder, "Think about the trout fishing." Her smile met me head-on, and I found it irresistible. It had been a long time since the concrete block enveloping me had let in a crack of light. Lisa had her hook in me.

CHAPTER THREE

The Aqua Blue staff Christmas party was elegant and crowded. Jorge, the chef from one of my other restaurants, came over to prepare the delectables for the staff. In addition, staff from the other restaurants traded Christmas party gigs so that everyone could enjoy their own party, from dishwashers, to bar staff, cooks, servers, and managers too. I was big on staff Christmas events, providing excellent food, entertainment, and drinks. This was my way of thanking everyone in my organization. Tonight was Aqua Blue's turn.

Staff Christmas parties were traditionally held on a Sunday evening after dinner service so as not to interfere with customer Christmas functions. Lisa sat at a table with one of the other hostesses, Jean, and the day-time bartender, Daisy. I stopped by to see if they were having a good time.

Daisy patted the seat at the table next to her. "Sit a minute."

I hesitated, but then I sat.

"Great party," Lisa said immediately.

"Yeah, Jorge did a great job," I replied.

Lisa was wearing a draped chiffon dress with dolman sleeves that looked like it might be vintage but was, I knew, the latest style. Her hair was up in a twist near the top of her head. She was a beautiful woman.

I looked to Jean, the other hostess. "So, Jean, what are you doing for the holiday?"

"Turkey for fourteen, and I still need to hit Toys"R"Us for my youngest. The usual zoo. What about you?"

I replied, "Actually, I'm a loner this Christmas. My wife is taking my son away to Taos. I think I'll probably go to a movie."

Lisa said, "Sounds like my life. Except I have the added benefit of taking the crowded metro to Westchester to see my parents. My sister comes with my nephew. Not that I don't love kids, but it's cartoons and action movies all day long, or else it's 'Aunt Lisa, take me on the snowboard,' or 'Aunt Lisa, can we take a ride on the sled?'" She lowered her head to mine and said, "You know, I saw some uniforms that are much better than the ones I showed you. I would like to show them to you."

I considered. "Okay. Let's do it after Christmas. You know I really appreciate how much interest you're taking in your job." I emphasized the "after Christmas" part, making sure that the meeting did not sound personal.

I noticed that Daisy and Jean had disappeared, and I was sitting alone with Lisa. This made me very uncomfortable as I felt a hundred eyes on me. I quickly stood. "Well, I've got to keep circulating. Have a wonderful Christmas." Before she could say another word, I melted into the thinning crowd.

A few days after Christmas, Lisa appeared at the door to my headquarters office. I looked at my watch, surprised to see her since we had no appointment. It was late in the afternoon if she was to make her evening shift.

"Are you going to work late?" I asked.

"No, it's my day off. I'm all yours."

I hailed a cab, and Lisa gave the Tocas address.

Once seated and handed menus, I looked at the uniforms the hostesses were wearing. I told her I thought the ones she designed were nicer.

The waitress came by to ask for our drink orders, and we looked blankly at her. I said, "Give us a moment or two."

When she'd left, I said nervously, "Would you like some dinner?"

"Sounds good to me."

We both ordered a glass of wine. I ordered the bass special, and Lisa ordered shrimp scampi. While we were dining and making small talk, my cell phone rang. I let my voicemail pick up and turned the phone off. Lisa followed my lead and did the same. Over a shared dessert, we talked about the restaurant business and why I loved it. Coffee and brandy brought conversation of Lisa's dream to get away from the city to raise a small family, and I told her how much I missed being part of a family myself.

It was probably four hours later when I checked my watch. "My God, I've got to go." I paid the check, which had been dropped off quite some time before.

Outside the restaurant, I offered to get Lisa a cab. I knew she lived somewhere uptown from her employee application. The first cab to come along stopped and pulled over.

Before Lisa folded herself into the cab, she stood close and said, "It's been a pleasure getting to know you, Mr. Bobby Lakeland."

And then she kissed me—not a New York kiss, but a lover's kiss goodnight.

Section II: The Net

CHAPTER FOUR

All the next day I tried like hell to concentrate on the P&Ls on my desk, but it wasn't happening. I just kept replaying the scene with Lisa in front of Tocas, the kiss that seemed to last a long time and say so much. I reviewed our conversation, turning over her words and remembering her perfume and what a great kiss that was. Then Bobby Lakeland "the boss" would come out and admonish me about not dating an employee, about the danger of sexual harassment cases. I could not put myself in that position. It would be suicide. In more than twenty years I never had an affair with an employee. But Lisa was the one really being aggressive and sending messages. But probably no woman looked litigious about sexual harassment—what would that look like, anyway? Then I'd think about the kiss, and the argument in my head would start all over again until finally I said aloud to all the voices in my head, "Stop!"

I took out her personnel sheet and noticed that she had put down her cell phone number and her mother's number. No apartment number. So, which did I call? I dialed the cell phone before I could lose my nerve, but an announcement came on saying that the service was interrupted. It was possible that she had switched services or something. That left her mother's number. Maybe I should call Information. I knew she had an apartment near the restaurant we visited last night. But something kept driving me, so I called her mother's number.

"Hello?" The woman who answered had a pleasant, young-sounding voice.

"Hello, I'm trying to reach Lisa Babcock, and her cell phone doesn't appear to be in service."

"Who is calling?"

"This is Bobby Lakeland; I hope I'm not disturbing anything."

"No, and Lisa is actually here. Hold on, and I'll get her for you."

I thought this was a good omen.

"Hello?"

"Lisa, it's Bobby here."

"Hi!"

"Nice that you're visiting with your mother. I couldn't reach you on your cell phone."

We had an inane conversation about her changing providers, and then without thinking through the consequences, I asked if she would meet me for a drink that night after work at Bloody Mary's.

Lisa dressed in an understated fashion. I was seated at a booth in the dark bar so I wouldn't be noticed if any staff from Aqua Blue happened to come in.

She looked lovely, and I told her so.

"And so do you." She smiled. I was, in fact, uneasy.

We ordered drinks. Lisa was completely in control. First she brought up the uniforms, asking about the progress I thought Hy was making. When that conversation was exhausted, she asked how my son was. Finally we had run out of small talk, and Lisa, as I would learn was her way, became very direct.

"Is something bothering you about this?"

I replied, "Well, I've never taken a staff member on a date before. I'm worried that we'll be seen."

"There's no one here that we know."

I went further with this conversation, being as direct as she was and being totally honest. I said I was worried that our having a drink would bleed into our working relationship and other employees might pick up on it. That could ruin the work atmosphere.

"Bobby, I have way too much respect for you to ever put you in a compromising position. I really like you. I see a very gentle, caring person that I admire and am attracted to. I would never embarrass you in any shape or form. I don't know if you've noticed, but I'm really physically attracted to you and want to get to know you better. Does that put you at ease?"

I brought the conversation back to business. "The staff at Aqua Blue would talk if they learned we had even one date. Restaurants thrive on gossip. I think all businesses do."

"No one has to know. I'm a great actress. And I don't talk about my business."

The waiter came to bring our third round of drinks. Neither of us had much interest in it. It was already two o'clock in the morning.

"I should go," Lisa said. "I hate to, but if I don't get enough sleep, I'm a bear the next day."

"Are you working tomorrow?"

She gave me a look I could not misinterpret and said, "Tomorrow is my day off."

I was still holding back. I felt a push and pull inside me, but Lisa led the way.

"Let's take advantage of it," Lisa said. She gave my hand a squeeze.

Outside I hailed a taxi for her. As it stopped, she gave her mouth to me in a kiss that tumbled down to my feet. She said, "You are a great kisser. Has anybody ever told you that?"

As she stepped back to leave, she said, "Tomorrow then?"

"Come to my apartment. We'll have dinner." I gave her my address. "Seven o'clock?"

The cab driver opened his window and said, "Are you coming? Because I am turning on my meter." His accent was Middle Eastern, and his English was very correct. We smiled at each other, and Lisa hopped in the cab without another word.

CHAPTER FIVE

I called down to the doorman to let him know about Lisa's expected arrival time and that there was no need to call up, just give her directions to my unit. All day I had been really excited about having Lisa at my condo. I left early to pick up a few things for our dinner. I was in the kitchen when I heard the knock on the door.

This evening she wore a red silk dress that clung to her curves. Black, strapped high heels completed the outfit.

I answered the door, and it occurred to me that it was the first time she had seen me in jeans. I was wearing a camel-colored cashmere sweater over a white T-shirt—very classic, but a little casual compared to Lisa's outfit.

I took her on a tour of the apartment, first the sunken living room with a huge bay window overlooking the cityscape. We could see Trump Plaza. The living room had hardwood oak flooring covered with an Oriental rug. The fireplace was lit, giving off a sensuous glow. The furniture was comfortable, soft nubuck and leather.

I stopped at the wet bar placed strategically in the window facing Second Avenue and offered her a drink. I poured myself a glass of cold sake, so she asked for the same.

The kitchen, small like all other New York kitchens, had been modernized with the latest appliances scaled down to New York City size. The metal gleamed. The granite counters were handsome. The white tiles were Italian.

"Let's eat," I said. I noticed how she was taking everything in, her eyes darting around the entire condo.

The kitchen stood conveniently as an open area between the living and dining rooms. I had renovated the apartment to make this possible. From the kitchen I brought out a platter of sushi, arranged in rows. I added a cold white wine to the bottle of sake. The table had already been set, and there was a vase of white roses. I could see that Lisa observed everything—the feel of the silver; the damask linen; and the eclectic collection of art and sculpture, including a bronze horse mounted on a pedestal with his nostrils flaring, midstride, an Arabian.

"I love that horse. Did you buy it in a museum shop?"

"Dave brought it back from Morocco as a gift for me. He bought it in the bazaar."

"Your apartment is quite beautiful. And I haven't even seen the whole thing. You have exquisite taste. No wonder the restaurants are so beautiful."

Lisa raised her glass and gave a toast, "To a wonderful evening." We clinked glasses.

As the dinner progressed, Lisa asked more questions about the apartment, the art, and the antiques. Dessert was almond gelato and fortune cookies. Mine was one of the silly ones that told me to pick a horse with winged feet or go hungry.

Lisa pretended to read hers and said, "Mine says, 'Look inside the bedroom.'"

I didn't think about it at all; I put my mind on hold and let myself be led by my senses. In the bedroom, Lisa was the one who hesitated, making a pretense of examining the room, shutters rather than blinds, the king-size bed, and a comforter covered by a beige, ruched duvet. She stopped to admire the various photos of my son, Jeff, taken at various ages and in different locations. "Oh, he's so cute, Bobby."

Lisa went to the bathroom off the bedroom, leaving me to decide where to put myself. I sat on the lounge chair next to the window that overlooked Seventy-ninth Street. It was dark and fairly quiet. Ordinarily, I would be reading or online, but right now all I could think about was the young woman in my condo.

She appeared. Her shoes were off. Lisa had my full attention. She raised one leg onto the bed and undid a garter, rolling down a stocking. Never had I seen such an act. I could not remember ever seeing a garter except the kind that brides throw at weddings. She kept her face intent on what she was doing, moving to the other leg and revealing the garter there attached to a stocking, repeating the motion of removing the stocking.

Bare-legged, she motioned to me and said, "Shoes and socks off. Just to be fair."

I removed my Tod's driving shoes and black wool socks.

Lisa did not hesitate. With one graceful motion, she removed her dress and looked me squarely in the eye. She was wearing a belt around her waist attached to garters, a fascinating piece of equipment that accentuated her trim waist and slightly rounded hips. Lisa reached her arms around herself and unhooked the garter belt, which fell to her feet alongside the dress.

Her lingerie was pure silk tap-dance panties, rose-colored, with a bra that scooped to her cleavage, boosting her breasts, offering them, the white skin revealed almost to her nipples. My eyes strayed down her body to the V between her legs.

I stripped hurriedly and went to her, kissing her lips, her neck, and moving her to the bed. I was not aware of much after that except that I was kissing this perfect body everywhere I could touch or lick or place my lips, and she was reciprocating. Lisa had a gentle touch, not in the least aggressive, nor was she diffident. With her hands and mouth, she located places on my body that I did not know were hot spots. We made love in a number of ways until I finally exploded. The orgasm was euphoric. Never had I experienced sex like that. If that was heroin, I understood addiction.

We both collapsed onto the bed. I was soaking in perspiration like I had just run a marathon. I was still trying to catch my breath. I looked at Lisa. I wanted to say something, but the only thing that came out was "Wow."

She replied, "Double wow."

I was wondering if I should ask her to stay the night. But Lisa surprised me. "I should leave," she said. She was already putting on her clothes.

"Listen, don't you ever take a day off, Bobby?"

"Yes, Saturday. What would you like to do?"

"Take a trip upstate with me. There's someone I want you to meet. Will you come?"

Oh, God, she was going to spring on me now the information that she had a child tucked away somewhere. But I did not hesitate. "Okay."

"It's a surprise. You'll be safe. No one will know us. Your anonymity will be protected." She said this last phrase in a mock serious tone.

This satisfied me. "See you Saturday, then."

"Stay right where you are so I can remember you like that. I'll let myself out." And she was out the door.

I collapsed on the bed. Pinching myself to make sure this was not a dream, I fell asleep.

CHAPTER SIX

The New York Thruway was fairly crowded, but I maneuvered around the clunky SUVs with my Toyota, and we reached Exit 20 within an hour from the George Washington Bridge. We had not discussed our destination. We listened to Whitney Houston's latest CD and let the time go by in quiet. When we reached the exit for Saugerties, I said, "Where to?"

Lisa pointed to Route 9W. "You are about to meet my baby boy." I guess the jig was up. She had a son. I sat quietly, thinking about how hard it must be for her to have farmed her son out. I could relate, as I didn't live with my son, and I felt for her. My question was who had she trusted him with...her sister, her parents, or perhaps the father?

I felt a bunch of complicated feelings well up inside me, but I figured I'd process them later. We drove through the town of Saugerties to an extremely rural area across the way from the Hudson. We stopped at a somewhat funky-looking house with a barn and a paddock behind it. As we approached closer, we saw a woman in the paddock, in shirtsleeves, jeans, and jodhpurs, giving a lesson to a child on a pony as the mother looked on. Beneath her black hat, the child had a huge smile.

Lisa called, "Hey, Beth," and kept walking. I followed her into the barn towards a stall around the corner from the others.

"This is my baby boy." The horse whinnied as we approached, nodding his huge brown head up and down as Lisa took an apple from her tote.

I started laughing and squeezed her waist. "You had me going there. Nice one, Lisa." She laughed and hugged me.

"His name is O'Brien."

With great relief, I examined the horse. I was, in truth, no horse lover. But at her urging, I put a hand on the soft, hazelnut-colored face and saw the horse's black eye studying me. Some of the white of his eye showed, and Lisa rubbed the horse's neck, calming him. She fed him the apple from her palm, O'Brien's whiskery nose gently removing the fruit. The look on Lisa's face was unmistakable. She was in love with her horse. Lisa looked natural, and in that state, she appeared to me as a gorgeous woman at home inside herself.

"Let's take him out to the paddock," she said.

I watched as she attached a lead to the horse's halter and led him through the muddy center of the stable out to an enclosed area where two geldings grazed. Lisa led him into the paddock and checked his body out, looking at his hooves and touching him, apparently making sure everything was sound. She clapped her hands, and the stallion moved with grace in a trot across the paddock.

Lisa leaned with her back against the fence, a cowgirl pose.

"So what do you think of my boy?"

"I don't know anything about horses, really. He's big."

"I bought him as a baby. My dream is to train him for national shows—maybe even the Olympics."

"Well, that's a terrific dream, and I hope you can make it real."

For a moment, I had a glimpse of Lisa astride me the night before, the grip of her as she was on top of me, how delicious she was.

She did not ride O'Brien. She took the horse back, gave him a kiss on his nose like she was a little girl, and we started our drive back to the city.

We cuddled in the car, holding hands as Lisa closed her eyes.

Once on the FDR Drive, I said to Lisa, "My house for dinner?"

"Sounds perfect."

This time Lisa sat at one of the counter seats along the island in the kitchen as I put together the ingredients for the stir-fry I was preparing. At dinner Lisa drew me out, asking questions about my marriage. It was hard to talk about it. I stayed focused on my seven-year-old son, Jeff.

"My son means everything to me."

"Where is your son now?"

"He lives with his mother in New Jersey. I see him every other weekend. It was not an amicable breakup, and we fought over custody. She won, and I lost."

As we had dinner—spring field salad and a seafood stir-fry on Shanghai noodles—Lisa continued peppering me with questions, but I said, "Lisa, let's change the subject."

The music changed to the new Bruce Springsteen CD, and Lisa talked about the women I had met at Bloody Mary's the first time we met, one she had grown up with, Nicole, who was now a legal secretary, and the other was named Katie. They were all friends from grade school. Lisa admitted that she found other women to be competitive and downright mean. As a result, she kept her distance and didn't get too close. These two were Lisa's only friends. I reminisced about the first time I heard "Born to Run," when I was a little older than Lisa was now. The subject of our age difference came up. Sooner or later we would have to deal with it, but not tonight.

"There's something I want to talk about before we take a step towards the bedroom," Lisa said.

I used the remote to turn the music down. The counter had been cleared of dishes, and we sat catty-corner and very close. She put one hand on my arm. "It's about contraception. I take the pill, and I've had an HIV test, so I don't like to use condoms. Is that okay with you?"

"That's a relief. I don't like them either."

"So let's go then." Lisa was pulling me off the stool towards the bedroom. I was thinking of her muscular thighs and perfect ass. "Let's spend the night together."

"I know that song," I said. I picked her up and carried her to the bedroom.

This night was not a repeat of our first time together. Rather, we were less inhibited with each other. Lisa did not give me a chance to make the first move; she moved me onto my back and started kissing the length of my body until her lips encircled my hard-on, and her tongue was knowing. When she had brought me to the tipping point, the licking ceased and she mounted me, her head thrown back, her shadow thrown against the wall. We came together.

The night moved with great luxury and feeling into the next morning. I stared at Lisa, thinking how close to perfection she was and how long it had been since I had this feeling. I wasn't going to think beyond the scent of Lisa in my bed, and the memory of last night. She was still asleep, curled up with the duvet over her, when I awoke at seven o'clock in the morning. Quietly, I removed myself from her embrace and went to the kitchen, determined to make an excellent cup of coffee.

CHAPTER SEVEN

The next evening I came into the restaurant at nine, gave a general smile to Lisa and the other woman at the hostess desk, and kept walking. Later I sat in Hy's office as we reviewed operational results, labor costs, and productivity.

Hyland Prescott was a veteran restaurateur and in his early fifties. He had worked twenty years for the Playboy Club corporation before they started their demise. I had a real respect for Hy. I loved his work ethic, his professionalism, and the pride he had in his operation. If there was a fault I could find with him, it was his inability to let go and allow others to manage. As a result, other managers frequently requested a transfer to one of the other restaurants to avoid working under Hyland Prescott. I usually put new managers and school trainees with him so he would feel less competition.

Hy had been with me for over three years, and when I signed the deal for this location and thought of the concept of Aqua Blue, Hy was my immediate choice to captain the ship.

"Okay, the restaurant is off to a good start, don't you think, Hy?"

"Yes. I'm happy if you're happy."

"How is the new reservation system for the hostesses working?"

Hy leaned back in this desk chair, pulling his styrofoam cup to him. Why the manager insisted on drinking Starbucks coffee when he had an entire elegant restaurant at his disposal was a mystery to me.

"The system is fine," he said, "but the hostesses don't get along with each other. I'm surprised you didn't smell the tension zone when you walked in. I'm always afraid there'll be a catfight."

I did not ask if Lisa was involved. I didn't want to know. Hy would handle it.

Dave Salzman's city home was a brownstone on Fifty-first between First and Second, which he had bought in the late eighties right after "Black October," during the crash in the market. The price was right. He had an architect redo the antiquated kitchen and added a closed-in patio that overlooked the garden. The formal living room was on the second floor, but right now the Super Bowl party was concentrated on the third floor, in the entertainment room where Dave's HD plasma TV was surrounded by a group of guys. Dave's Super Bowl parties were sacrosanct, guys only. I believed he did this so he could smoke his Cuban cigars without worrying about the odor, though I had met several women in the last few years who smoked them as well. Right now Salzman was smoking some huge, smelly thing that must have cost forty dollars.

It was halftime between the Cowboys and the Bills. The game was close, with the Cowboys slightly ahead. A female rap artist was singing, someone I did not know. On his way down to check on the caterer in the kitchen, Dave passed by me and said, "Hey, there you are. You look great, man."

"I'm seeing someone. I guess it shows."

"Anyone I know?"

"Yes, in fact, you recommended her."

Dave stopped his forward motion toward the stairs. "The blonde from Bloody Mary's? The Aqua Blue babe? She's hot!"

"Let me walk downstairs with you," I said. "I want to talk to you about something."

The hallway was forest green with the original dark-oak banister leading down to the first floor. When we got to the kitchen, the caterer was placing tiny pizzas and chicken kabobs on platters. Satisfied, Dave led me into the sitting room to the right of the front door, a real man's room with dark leather appointments and walls of bookshelves.

"What's up?" he asked. "I don't want to miss the third quarter."

"Well, I've never dated an employee before. It's a little strange. She's a fabulous woman. It's way beyond sex, though the sex is the best I've ever had."

Dave held his hands palms out, as though to reign me in. "Hold on there, just hold on. Why doesn't she quit the job?"

"She likes it. And she's an asset."

"You're playing with fire, Bobby. Try to find her another job outside of your company. You have lots of connections."

"Lisa's not like that; she's like a cowgirl, very wholesome. She's not your typical Manhattan man-eater."

"Bobby, listen to you. You sound like your brains have turned to mush over this woman."

"Wait a minute. You were the one who suggested I date her. It seems to me it was me who mentioned sexual harassment. Now the roles have changed?"

"Yeah, but I didn't think you'd go mad about her. It can go bad," he said. "But if she works for you, it can get really bad."

Dave shook his head. From all the way upstairs came the sound of men making the sound they make only when sports are involved. "Okay, I've said my piece."

I thought about this as we walked up the stairs. I didn't feel like going back to the game. Here I had thought Dave would be encouraging, and he was making me more nervous. Well, the best thing for me to do was keep my own counsel about Lisa. I knew she wouldn't like it if I removed her from the job. She would see it as me doubting her trustworthiness, which it would be. What a terrible way to start a relationship. I wasn't going to say anything. Not now, anyway.

On Monday there was a managers' meeting at Aqua Blue. I found Lisa at the front desk when I arrived and assumed she was working a double shift. I gave her a smile that I thought was professional, though it was not exactly my formal look. Lisa kept her cool, but I sensed the other hostesses checking us out.

The managers had arrived for the meeting, and we all sat down at a table in the back of the restaurant.

Twice a year, we get all the general managers, dining room managers, and culinary managers and have a full day of operational reviews by restaurant. With Aqua Blue, this brought the total to five restaurants in our family. The format for the day consisted of each general manager recapping the latest operational results, reporting on any trends, and discussing what projects they were working on.

As each restaurant concept was different, I approached this as a collection of independent restaurateurs working for the same company. Lakeland Restaurants paid out two levels of bonuses to the management. One was based on individual restaurant results, and the second bonus was based on the overall performance of the entire company. This way, all managers had a vested interest in the entire company and not just their own units.

In the afternoon, we brainstormed based on various operational problems. I always prepared a list of new restaurants in the vicinity worth discussing based on menus, operational procedures, policies, and promotional programs. I always looked forward to these meetings. They gave everyone a forum to discuss matters and to seek advice from peers.

By five o'clock the meeting was finished, and the managers were off to their own restaurants. After I had a few words with the newest manager, a woman recently graduated from Cornell, I found Hy in the kitchen observing the wait staff. I wasn't sure why. The kitchen was a cacophony of banging cookware, voices raised to order, cursing, and the constant sound of percussive Latin music. And it was hot. I loved restaurant kitchens, as did Hy—something we shared. After all, you don't have a restaurant without a kitchen.

I asked Hy to step outside. When we were in a quiet place, I asked if the hostess situation had cleared up.

"Yes. I don't know why, but the girls seem to be less acrimonious."

"That's good, Hy. Let me know if you have any more problems."

In reality, I was hoping that Hy would take care of my situation with Lisa for me. That way I could recommend her to another restaurant outside of the company. I was close with Hy, but I wouldn't involve him in my personal life.

Section III: The Snag

Four Months Later

CHAPTER EIGHT

As spring approached and the city was warming, I found my relationship with Lisa cooling. After five months of dating, the sudden change in her was bewildering to me. It started when I returned from Florida with David. At first I thought she was pissed off that I went away for two weeks with my friend, even though I had spoken to her practically every day. She was spending more time upstate with O'Brien and had less time for me. I did not believe she was seeing another man, but something was definitely wrong.

I knew Lisa was heading up to Saugerties, and I wanted to see her before she left. I could not believe how much I had grown to depend on seeing her, and making love to her, over the past five months. I felt like an addict. I did not understand what was eating her, but I had to find out to make it right. I tried the restaurant, hoping she would answer the phone, but one of the other hostesses answered, so I clicked off without saying anything.

This was ridiculous. I was acting like a child. I decided to confront her in the restaurant. I couldn't believe how this was affecting me. It was as if nothing else mattered. I was just focused on this aspect of my life. I had the presence of mind to chide myself for acting like a schoolboy who had an all-encompassing crush on a classmate. But that didn't avert my mission. I hopped in a cab and decided to confront her at Aqua Blue.

When I arrived, Lisa was not up front, but I saw her leading people to a table, and my eyes followed her progress through the restaurant.

Finally she was facing me.

"Hi, Bobby," she said, like nothing was wrong and my world wasn't coming apart.

"Lisa, what's wrong?"

"Nothing. What are you talking about?" Her voice sounded distant.

How could I explain the inexplicable? I looked around, realizing we might gain an audience. "Will you meet me tonight after work?"

She hesitated. "Okay, eleven thirty at Mary's?"

At eleven thirty I was at a table, drumming my fingers and watching the clock. I had a double scotch in front of me, and as I took a swallow, Lisa walked through the door. What I could not have known was that before she arrived, she had reviewed this **tête-à-tête** with her friend Nicole, who had given her "marching instructions" for the evening: "Don't sleep with him, whatever you do." Later in our relationship, Lisa got tipsy and gave me some insight into Nicole's advice on romance. It seems this dating maven, as she saw herself, had counseled Lisa to make herself seem unavailable at this time in order to make me nervous. I am horribly embarrassed to say it worked. The conflict between men's common sense and their emotional balance is confounding.

I smiled nervously as she approached the table. The waitress came over, and I ordered Lisa an apple martini, but Lisa stopped me. "No, I'll just have wine. I don't want to drink too much. I have to get home early." She looked at me to see if I would respond.

"What's up with you, Lisa?" I asked when the server had gone. "Don't say there's nothing going on. I'm too old to waste time with half-truths in a relationship. Why are you so distant? Are you angry that I went to Florida with David?"

Lisa seemed to be thinking this over.

"Lisa? Are you going to answer?"

"It's not that I mind you going away with Dave, not really. I mind being apart from you. I mind sleeping with you and then going home to a different apartment. I don't like the roller coaster of being intimate with someone but seeing them so sporadically. I would rather not have the relationship at all. It's too painful to be up and down like this."

"What does that mean, Lisa? Did I do something that you perhaps misinterpreted? What can we do to put it right?"

"I don't know, Bobby. Let's let it marinate awhile."

"Marinate?"

"You know, let's sleep on it."

"Okay, let's sleep on it at my place."

Lisa smiled, put on her coat, and kissed me on the cheek. "No, we need to think about it separately. I'll call you."

As she walked out the door, I realized she had seized the ball. She'd call me? This was starting to get me frustrated, even a little angry. I didn't like to be played. Maybe Dave was right after all. When we were down in Florida, Dave talked about the relationship progression, asking if Lisa was pressuring for the next step. Now I understood what he was talking about.

CHAPTER NINE

My cell woke me up. Every time it rang over the last two days, I rushed to check the caller ID, hoping it was Lisa. When it wasn't, I crashed. The full meaning of "crestfallen" became apparent to me. My shield was down, and I felt vulnerable and whipped.

"Hey, we're late, buddy!" Dave sounded so upbeat I wanted to strangle him.

"Late for what?"

"Hey, Lakeland, get your head on straight. We're in the club tennis doubles championship today, remember?"

Oh no, I couldn't. I just could not play a game of doubles, never mind a championship.

"Where are you?" I asked.

"I'm on my way in from Dix Hills. One hour. I'll swing over and pick you up."

I crawled through the motions; I showered, not bothering to shave. If I were a praying man, I might have asked for some strength. The cell rang again.

"Hey, amigo, I'm downstairs. What's taking you so long? It's time to win that trophy."

I threw on my white tennis shirt and shorts, tied my Geox tennis shoes, grabbed my jacket, and caught the elevator.

Dave was in front of the building in his red convertible Mercedes SL. Ordinarily, I would have appreciated the comfort of the red leather seats and the roof down in April, but today I was silent and felt the cold.

"You look like shit," said Dave. "You sick or something?"

"Something. I had a lot to drink and didn't sleep well."

"Is it something Lisa can fix?" Dave asked in a rambunctious tone.

"Actually, Lisa is the reason I feel like crap."

Dave gave me a compassionate look. "Women. We'll talk after the game. You feel okay to play?"

I would not back out of something that meant so much to Dave. "Sure. Let's eat them for lunch."

The club was located midtown and supplied valet parking to its own lot. Members paid dearly for the privilege, but as they say, membership has its advantages.

The inside courts felt overly warm. We practiced a warm-up set on one of the open courts.

"Who are we playing first?" I asked.

"Last year's doubles champs, Eddy and John. We're going to have to dig deep here. Eddy has a wicked-fast serve, and John is supposed to be really sneaky, good strategy."

I groaned inwardly. I had a pain in my arm and thought I might have pulled a muscle.

Dave and I knew each other's moves and usually made a great team, but today I was totally off. I was out of breath by the middle of game one, which Eddy and John won immediately. I couldn't imagine why I was so exhausted. By game two, John obviously noticed my vulnerability because he kept playing every ball to me, making me chase them—and his strategy was working. Third game, same thing. The first set went to John and Eddy without a fight.

As we switched sides, Dave said, "Hey, are you okay? You're playing for shit."

"I'm trying, Dave. I have heartburn or something—too much rum and Diet Coke last night."

The game went on like that, with me huffing and puffing and Dave trying to cover for me. They were ahead five games to none.

Dave said, "This is it—we do or die!"

We were eliminated six to nothing. I could only think about how glad I was that it was over.

"Jeez, we got scorched. Let me buy you breakfast," Dave offered.

"No, thanks, I'm going to catch a cab and get home to bed."

"You sure you don't want me to drive you?"

I shook my head. "Enjoy yourself. Take a steam. Don't let your day get totally wrecked. I need some sleep, that's all."

I asked the doorman to get me a cab, but when he returned to say the cab was waiting, I was sitting down.

"Mr. Lakeland, the cab is here, but you don't look so good."

"No, I'm okay." I tried to get up, but my stomach fell somewhere down below my knees, and my head seemed to weigh a hundred pounds. I sat and put my head between my knees.

"Listen," Henri said, "it's probably nothing, but why don't you ask the cab to take you to the hospital. I'll tell Mr. Salzman."

The doorman did not let me say another word. He knew I was ill, and he sure as hell did not want me to collapse on club grounds. Henri fed me into the taxicab.

"Take him to whatever hospital is closest, to the emergency room," Henri instructed the driver.

Luckily, the driver had been driving long enough to know the city streets. He drove me immediately to Lenox Hill Hospital.

I struggled to pay the driver and make it to the ER. I was more exhausted than I could ever remember feeling. In the back of my mind, I knew something was wrong. The triage nurse took my information and vital signs and immediately got me into a room and on a heart monitor. I gave in to my fatigue and for the next few hours felt only pokes and mild intrusions. The sound of people moving in and out of the room only mildly disturbed my sleep. Finally, I awoke to find an Indian doctor reading my chart and checking the monitor. A nurse was fooling around with one of the intravenous lines. It looked like she might be feeding something into it.

"What time is it?" I asked.

"It's three o'clock. I am Dr. Shanan. We are waiting for the result of your lab tests."

"Can't I go home, and you can call me with the results? I have a great doctor."

"Mr. Lakeland, you can do whatever you like—we don't run a prison here at Lenox Hill—but you have had a cardiac infarction."

"No. I'm forty-one years old. You're telling me I had a heart attack?"

"I have to see the results of your blood tests so the enzymes will confirm, but I am almost certain from the EKG." He took a piece of paper and showed me the blip in my heart rhythms.

"You really need to be admitted to this hospital and seen by one of our cardiologists."

Everything in me knew this doctor was right, but I couldn't absorb the information, nor could I surrender. A wave of depression overwhelmed me. What would life be like as a cardiac patient? Memories of my father's premature death came to me, unbidden.

"Is there someone we can call for you?"

I thought of Lisa and then rejected the thought. Not after last night. She was busy marinating. I gave the doctor Dave's cell phone number.

Time went by. It's impossible to know how much time. But when I woke up, Dave was seated next to me, and he looked worried.

"Hey, you're scaring me, boy. They want you to stay here for a few days. Can I go home and get you some stuff?"

The doctor and a nurse's aide came into the space, ready to wheel me to the CICU.

"Give us some information, will you pal?" Dave asked the doctor. Dave said he had been at my bedside for an hour, and this was the first he had seen of any medical staff.

"Your friend has definitely had a heart attack—not horrible, but it will require some lifestyle adjustments."

Then he addressed me. "We want you to rest, just as though you had broken a bone, and we will get you on the road to mending. You must rest for six weeks while your heart repairs. You'll have lots of instruction about what to eat and all of those things while you are here."

The nurse's aide, a black man in green scrubs, had the only smile in the room. In a Jamaican accent he said to me, "I will wheel you now. You'll be safe there. No troubles."

Dave asked me, "What do you need, and who should I call?"

"Um, call Lisa. Maria, my housekeeper, will be there tomorrow. I'll call her and tell her what to pack. If you could just pick up whatever she puts into a gym bag and bring it, that will be great. I think I'll be sleeping for a while."

"Anybody else? Your managers? Anybody at the restaurants?"

"I can't think right now, Dave. If you'll make those calls, I can deal with the rest tomorrow. Thanks, bro."

"Okay, man, but get some sleep. I need you to stick around awhile." Dave gave my hand a squeeze, and I realized he was really upset. Dave had been a good friend to me for years, and for some reason my eyes filled with tears. I was embarrassed to be weepy over nothing.

"God, how ridiculous," I said.

"That's okay, my father had a heart attack, and he got real weepy for a few weeks. It passed. No biggie. See you later."

I was wheeled out of the ER and into a brightly lit unit two floors up. That's all I remember. The next thing

I knew, Lisa was walking to my bedside with my gym bag on her arm. Perhaps it was a dream, I was thinking, wondering if they had given me any medication that might cause hallucinations.

"Bobby!" She was dressed in black jeans and a black top, and I wondered if I had died already and this was life after death. Lisa sat next to me on the bed, trying to grasp my shoulders. "Oh, Bobby, I'm so worried about you."

No, this was definitely Lisa. I could tell by her scent, which could not be conjured up. And the tears were for real. I was overcome by her concern and emotions.

"I'm going to take such good care of you."

"I take it you've marinated on this subject."

"Please don't tease. This is very serious. You could have died," she said.

I stayed quiet, forcing Lisa to look into my face.

"If it makes you this upset," she said, "I promise I won't do it again."

I smiled. It wasn't easy because I was doped up with something and totally not myself, but I managed a weak grin.

Lisa tried to get her arms around my neck, pushing around tubes and wires that were hooked up to me. A beeper sounded.

"I don't think you're supposed to do that," I said. "This is really sensitive equipment."

Within one minute a nurse was standing by my bed, frowning at both of us.

"Just testing the time it takes to get medical attention," I said, giving the nurse my most charming smile.

"Only kidding. My girlfriend set off the equipment by accident."

Girlfriend? Did I just say girlfriend?

"Both of you must be quiet. There are other patients. And you, Mr. Lakeland, can only have a visitor for fifteen minutes."

Before the nurse could throw her out, Lisa leaned down and whispered in my ear, "When I heard you were sick, I realized how much I want to be with you. I love you, Bobby. I freaked out when Dave told me you had a heart attack. Ask him, I was crazed. But now it's going to be alright. You'll see. I'm going to quit my job and help you get well."

I wasn't really sure what she meant or why it included quitting her job, but I was definitely not myself, not thinking clearly, and not in a position to ask too many questions. The nurse got Lisa out of the room with one evil-eye stare, and I went to sleep again.

When I awoke, Lisa was back in the room, and the doctor was there—this time a different doctor, a woman. "Good evening, Mr. Lakeland. I'm Dr. Cohen, your cardiologist." She turned to Lisa. "Are you a relative?"

"She's my sister," I said, before Lisa could say anything.

"Okay, as you know, you'll be here for five days. Then you must rest. We'll have you up and walking before you leave here. We don't recommend that patients stay in bed like in the old days, but you cannot go back to your old schedule for a while, and you'll need someone at home to take care of things."

I was thinking I could hire Maria for the full day to shop and cook. But when I looked at Lisa, I realized something was going on in her mind.

"I'm going to quit the job at Aqua Blue and take care of you."

"What about O'Brien, the love of your life?"

"We'll think of something. They'll probably let me drive you up there." Lisa turned to the doctor and said, "He'll be able to take rides into the country, right?"

"So long as he doesn't drive, that will be fine. He'll know exactly what his own limits are."

I started thinking about being away from work for six weeks.

"Okay, young lady, you should leave, give Mr. Lakeland some rest."

"I'll be back tomorrow, Bobby," Lisa said to me.

CHAPTER TEN

I came home to a heart-attack-free zone. And I came home to Lisa. She had moved herself into my apartment, even set up a closet for herself in the bedroom. I had just enough energy to make it into the master bathroom, where I saw the makeup and unguents that told me there was definitely a woman in residence. She coaxed me into an easy chair in the living room, gave me the remotes to the plasma television and the sound system, and left to make a bite to eat. I have to say I was touched. It had been a long time since anyone had taken care of me—that is, anyone who had not been paid to do so. Lisa had thought through all the necessities of caring for my every need. She had gone out and purchased wooden TV trays and set up a bowl of what she told me later was organic, fat-free, sodium-free vegetable soup with whole-wheat crackers and "healing tea." She was so proud of herself that I could not help but be won over. By the time the meal was over, I started to feel as if I was truly loved.

I woke, thankful to be in my own apartment. My six days in the hospital scared the hell out of me. Two men had died while I was in intensive care. My own mortality had introduced itself, and it scared me.

Lisa was at my side. She checked her watch and noticed it was time to take one of my blood thinners. The medications were meticulously placed on a table next to the bed. She put a bottle of Evian and glass within my reach, and she asked, "Are you hungry?"

"Lisa, I'm fine, really."

She ran down the list of things I was supposed to do before the day was over and reminded me not to cross my legs or raise my arms above my head. I was watching her and wondering where this Lisa came from, lovely and nurturing.

"Okay, Nurse Ratchet. I am under your complete control."

Her look was perplexed, and I realized she was too young to remember *One Flew Over the Cuckoo's Nest*, and I was too tired to explain. "Never mind, it's from an old book."

She fussed over the duvet and asked me if I would rather be in a chair in the living room. When she saw that I was settled, Lisa went to start "a heart-friendly dinner."

"Lisa, thank you, really. You're the best."

The smile she gave me was full of meaning, but I couldn't read her right then. I was tired. I slept.

Lisa used Dr. Ornish's cookbook, measuring carefully. She had purchased all the right ingredients the day before. I was up and about the apartment. I wandered into the kitchen.

"Smells good in here."

"It's a recipe from Dr. Ornish's book. It sounds good. I think even a gourmet like you might like it."

Her nurturing drew me closer. This was a trait my wife never had—not even for our child. I felt myself creeping close to that line that had kept me from falling head-over-heels in love.

In truth, the meal was horrible, and I made a mental note to figure out a way to relieve Lisa of kitchen duty without hurting her feelings. But I complimented her anyway, saying the meal was tasty.

"I'm glad you like it. I'm not much of a cook."

"I never would have known!" I smiled. Luckily she didn't know I was teasing.

Dessert was worse than dinner—a baked apple with no sugar or sweetener. But I found I was really hungry, and I ate it anyway. After dinner Lisa cleared the table, and we drank a second glass of merlot—just what the doctor ordered. My entire perspective on life had altered, as anyone's might, and I spoke of my brush with death. Lisa was too young to truly empathize, but she looked serious at the right places. This prompted me to open up even more. I had been betrayed by my body, and now I knew that my life, like everyone's, was fragile and could be taken from me at any moment. I described my frustration and sadness that I could not see my son more often. I confided in her the story of my first marriage. One day my wife just decided things weren't working and wanted a divorce. She got full custody of our child after a long and expensive trial. There was nothing I could do at the time. I was working nonstop to build my business. The custody laws are drawn up to give full custody to the primary caregiver.

When I came to a stop in the story, I was as exhausted as I've ever been.

Lisa put her hand on my arm and said, "You're safe with me, Bobby. You never have to worry."

Surprising myself, I said, "I love you, Lisa." The words sounded right on my lips. I said them again. "I love you."

Section IV: The Trap

CHAPTER ELEVEN

By May I was feeling like myself again. Actually, I was feeling better. I had heard guys say a major illness could open your eyes to how you lived your life, and I always figured it was good for them, but not for me. How wrong I was. I was conscientious about working out at the club—even had the trainer there work out a program for me. I avoided stress, which is pretty hard in the restaurant business, and I disciplined myself to let the managers make more decisions and to be sure and take a few days off each week. And God help me, I began to meditate—not one of those strange, new age practices, just tuning in to my breathing. It worked. My blood pressure was lower than it had been in years. Life was good, maybe even the best time of my life. I really did feel safe with Lisa, especially now that she wasn't working at Aqua Blue. Even my son seemed happier to see me on our visits. Perhaps Jeff had on some level understood that his father was really sick and he might lose me.

When Lisa told me she was pregnant, the upward climb of this spiral came twirling down. I am not sure what I said exactly, but it was definitely not what she expected. Sure, I wanted a family, but not as a surprise barely five months into a relationship with a much younger woman. And not right after suffering a heart attack.

"I thought you were on the pill. That's what you told me."

"I stopped taking it. It was giving me headaches, and I wanted to be available for all your needs."

"Are you sure? I mean, how did you find out?" I said.

"I did a home pregnancy test, and then I saw my doctor." After a pause, she asked, "You don't want a family, Bobby? That's all you were talking to me about after you got out of the hospital—how much you had taken things for granted and really missed having a family. That's why I went off the pill—for you, Bobby, so you can have your family." Lisa put her face in the pillow and started crying.

###

Dave and I had picked up our tennis games, so when we met that weekend at the club, I was happy to move from the doubles we set up to the lunch we always shared afterward. Dave took a seat next to me at our table. I had already ordered a club soda. Dave wiped the sweat from his brow with his sports towel and signaled to the waitress that he wanted a Stella.

"These young guys are killing me," Dave said. "I'm not playing singles against them anymore. Thanks, sugar," he said to the waitress when she deposited his beer.

"What's the matter, Bobby?" Dave asked as he took a sip from the bottle.

I told him about Lisa. He had the audacity to ask me if I was surprised. I put down my glass with a bit too much force, and the waitress reappeared, thinking I wanted another. I smiled and waved her away.

I ran through it all with Dave—how she went off the pill, how ambivalent I felt—the whole deal. Dave surprised me by asking how Lisa felt, which hadn't occurred to me.

"She's surprised I'm not delirious with joy. Maybe she's right. I don't know. I'm totally fucked up about it. I should go to a shrink to figure out how I feel." I cracked a smile.

"My God, don't do anything rash. Let's talk about it. Why do you think she didn't talk to you about giving up the pill?"

"I want to believe what she's saying—that's how screwed up I feel."

"Yeah, denial is a great tool, but you have to deal with reality."

"Part of me is a little excited—I have to admit that."

"You need to sort this out before you go home and face Lisa."

CHAPTER TWELVE

Lisa arrived home after me. It was clear that she had been riding. I had gotten used to the smell of horse and even grown to like it. But right then I wondered how she could be pregnant and still go riding.

"How are you, baby?" Lisa gave me a kiss.

"I'm fine. Did you ride O'Brien?"

"Yes."

"Did you check with a doctor about whether that's advisable?"

"Why would I do that?"

"Lisa, if you're going to have a baby, it's no longer just you. You have to take into consideration that you're responsible for another life—in everything you do."

"So our baby will love riding." She gave me a goofy smile, and I was annoyed.

"I suggest you ask the doctor before you go riding again."

"Well, I'm glad you have concern for our baby." Lisa sat next to me on the couch, turning to look me full in the face. "How do you really feel, Bobby? I mean, we haven't talked." Her eyes were baby blue, a color I associated with fine silk or the iridescent sheen of a great fish catching the sun as it leapt out of the water. Was she asking me for honesty or just to hear what she wanted to hear?

"Well, I'm still in shock," I said.

"I know, but you said you wanted a family."

Did I say that? I wasn't sure. I had said I missed my son, the feeling of being a father. "Well, this is sort of premature, out of sequence. I didn't mean starting right now."

"So you don't want the baby. That's just great." Then she went into one of those lines it's really hard to forget because it's so classic: "I got pregnant for us, Bobby, because you were so sad about losing your other family. I thought this was what you wanted, and now you're blaming me, telling me I trapped you."

"I didn't say any such thing."

"You don't have to say it. You're thinking it."

"I just wish we had discussed it. It would've been nice to have some input." I paused. "Maybe a little forewarning."

"Forewarning! Did you and your wife plan exactly when she would get pregnant? Did you have forewarning? Or did she mean more to you than I do? No wonder she treated you like shit. You are shit."

I held up one hand, palm out. "Wait a minute…"

She stood, pointed to her body, and said she wasn't looking forward to being pregnant at twenty-four. Then she brought up another foxy argument—that I had never mentioned birth control, and since she was the one who had thought about it, she didn't have to ask me if she decided to stop using it. Lisa should have been a personal injury lawyer. I'm paraphrasing here, but she said something like, "Do you think you can control everything I do? Because that's what this is about for you, Bobby—you just want control."

"Lisa, sit down. I never said I didn't want the baby." I thought quickly. "Let me get you a glass of water. Maybe you should call your mom or one of your girlfriends and calm down a little. You're acting crazy." The truth was I did not want to deal with her like this. This was a side of her I had never seen.

"I won't sit down, and you can forget about the baby. We don't need you. I'll go back to work, find a place to live, and have the baby on my own. Then we'll see how much you like not being able to see another child." I could tell from the vicious glint in her eyes that she knew exactly how precise this verbal punch was.

With the last jab landed, she went into the bedroom and slammed the door.

In that short half hour, I resigned myself to living without Lisa. Honestly, there was a great deal of relief. Obviously, she was immature, certainly not mother, or wife, material. And I would be lucky to be out of the relationship. If she was determined to go through with the birth, I'd deal with it then, but there was no telling what she would do.

Just as I sat down for a cup of decaf and a plate of fruit, the bedroom door opened, and a completely different woman than the one who had slammed the door emerged. If I did not know Lisa, I would have thought she was schizophrenic.

"I'm sorry, Bobby. I didn't mean anything I said. My hormones must be getting the best of me."

I gestured for Lisa to join me, getting her a mug and the half-and-half for her coffee.

Lisa spoke to my back. "I love you. That's why I want your baby. No other reason. I know it looks like I'm trying to trap you, but I'm not. In fact, I'll sign anything you put in front of me—a prenup, whatever."

I shot her a look. A prenup? Who had mentioned marriage? She got my point.

"Well, not that," she said, "but anything that removes your obligation. I don't know the legal terms. The point is, even if I went to a clinic and picked out a donor, I would want my baby to have all of your character traits— your personality, brains, creativity, your fabulous smile. I just want us to be a family, to take care of you and now the baby. Please give it a chance. If it doesn't work, I'll take full custody of the baby, or give you partial custody or whatever you want, and I'll go."

I looked at humble Lisa and realized that this was who I loved. I quickly forgot the antics of twenty minutes ago.

It occurred to me that I had no idea what her mother and father were thinking about all this, and when I asked her, she cooed about how her mother couldn't wait to be a grandmother and that her parents were anxious to meet me.

She was getting to me. No doubt about it. Lisa could see this, though I hadn't moved a muscle. She was speaking to my male ego and to the part of me that did love her.

My attorney, Ken Wandrow, had represented me in business matters and personal real estate closings for the past fifteen years. Over this time we became friends, meeting for the occasional drink after work hours. Every year Ken invited me to his company Christmas party. Ken was a great attorney with a mellow personality. When I was divorcing my wife, I had asked Ken to represent me. He sent me to another lawyer in the practice. I suspected he'd do the same now, but I wanted to hash the situation out first with Ken.

I sat in the chair on the opposite side of Ken's glass and steel desk, which was as neat and uncluttered as the attorney's mind. I described the entire relationship with Lisa from the beginning.

"What's the best way to handle it?" I asked him. "Tell me what you really think."

"Bobby, you know I don't practice family law. There's an attorney I know, a sole practitioner. His name is William Drexler. He's not far from Aqua Blue, actually. He'll be able to handle your case better than I could." Ken checked his Rolodex and wrote a number on his card. "But since Lisa said she'd sign anything, my opinion is you should give her something to sign."

"Thanks, Ken."

CHAPTER THIRTEEN

We chose a Tuesday night for the meet-the-parents dinner. I wasn't nervous so much as on edge. I drove my car with the top up to avoid the smog and stench that hovers over the Cross Island Expressway from all the fumes of the jammed-up trucks and SUVs blowing gas. Lisa and I hadn't been talking much the last week. I still did not know how I felt about the baby. Drexler was on my calendar for the next week. I felt that anything I said would be wrong. God only knew what Lisa was thinking. She was fawning and overly indulgent. She was very aggressive in bed. But I was sensing something beneath this behavior, a kind of salesmanship.

"What are your parents' names again?" I asked.

"Darlene and Ernest. Babcock, in case you've forgotten my last name." She smiled. "Just relax, Bobby. They're nice people. They won't bite."

"I am relaxed. I just never got a girl in the family way before marriage and had to face her father. Not to mention that I'm probably almost his age."

"My father will love you. You can talk about the sixties."

"Let's see, in the sixties I was in high school. Where was he?"

"I don't know, ask him. Probably in Vietnam."

"That doesn't sound like a good discussion."

We pulled up a tree-lined driveway to a charming arts and crafts bungalow with cedar shingles and a large front porch. It was not what I had expected. Lisa's description of her parents' house had not been complimentary at all. I was pleasantly surprised in the feel and character of their dwelling.

Lisa's mother came to the door to greet us. When I tried to shake her hand, she pulled me to her and gave me a hug. I tried not to resist. Her blonde hair was exactly the same color as Lisa's, though her face was showing signs of wear with wrinkles around her mouth and between her eyebrows. Her neck was falling, but her body was in very good shape, I noticed. As they say, always look at a woman's mother... The jeans she wore were a size seven and very expensive, and they were topped by a scarlet cashmere cardigan belted at the waist. A shirt peeked out from beneath the sweater. I would have bet she wasn't wearing a bra. Darlene was probably fifty years old. She was just a few years older than me.

Darlene led us to the living room, where Ernest was coming in from the backyard. The living room picked up the style of the house, with a fireplace and a wood mantle, wood floors, and huge windows letting in the light. Ernie Babcock was unexpectedly big—not tall, but built solid. I tried to remember what he did for a living. We shook hands, and Babcock avoided looking me straight in the eye. The look spoke of many things, not all of them good. This man would not be easy to win over, if I wanted to win him, and I was ambivalent about my own goals for the evening.

Darlene offered me a cocktail, which I declined. Ernie suggested I join him at the barbecue, which he had already started outside. The two of us went out and threw a salmon on the grill.

"Wow, that smells great," I said. "What did you season the salmon with?"

"A little basil, dill, oregano, garlic, salt and pepper."

"Excellent," I said.

"So I can cook in one of your restaurants?"

We both laughed and felt the tension easing a little.

At the table, salad was served—mixed greens with lentils, berries, and nuts. I complimented them on everything. I was beginning to feel like a suitor, and it made me uneasy. I noticed Lisa said very little.

We made small talk. I told them I thought their house was wonderful. Ernie seemed to relax a little and began to ask me questions about myself and how I got started in business. By the time we got to dessert, we were having a real conversation. Over tea and a decidedly decadent cake from Bakery for the Best, the talk turned to the baby.

"So how do you really feel about this?" Ernie asked me.

"Shocked. A bit nervous."

"Me too," Lisa said.

Darlene finished serving the cake, and before anyone could comment, I changed the subject, asking Ernie about his work.

"You know, I never fulfilled my potential, as far as I'm concerned. I wanted to go to college, but Darlene got pregnant, and that was that." Ernie kept his eyes on the plate. He was probably about sixty, nineteen years older than me. How bizarre.

"Yeah, I never kind of caught up with my dreams," he said. "I've been a laborer all my life and could never get my foot in the white-collar door. Now you are something, a real model of success."

I was surprised that Ernie seemed to be putting himself down and putting me up on some kind of pedestal. My ex-wife's father had always looked down on me as an inferior.

"Well, I do plenty of labor, believe me, Ernie."

The four of us bid each other goodnight at the door, and Darlene said she hoped I would come back "before the baby's born" to visit.

On the way home, Lisa snuggled next to me in the car and said, "Gee, they really liked you."

"They're very nice people. I'm sure they will make great grandparents."

Lisa enthusiastically smiled at me. "I love you, Bobby. I'm so glad I'm having your baby."

CHAPTER FOURTEEN

A few months passed. Lisa could no longer avoid the bump that led her around. Maybe Angelina Jolie or Katie Holmes could look gorgeous while pregnant, but at six months Lisa felt fat and matronly. And I wasn't available much to reassure her. I had been involved in renovating one of my restaurants, and it required a great deal of my time. I'd already resumed my workaholic schedule, and this new project only added to it. The six weeks away just made the pile on my desk that much larger. Lisa and I hardly saw each other. She had been warned not to ride because her balance would be off at this point, and a fall would most likely cause her to miscarry. So she was totally bored. Her partying friends, Nicole and Katie, were having fun, going on dates and meeting for drinks, which, of course, Lisa couldn't do because she couldn't drink and meeting in a bar was too tempting.

Usually I dragged myself in at nine thirty or so, having already eaten dinner. One evening I was so tired when I got home I did not get past the living room, but I dropped an envelope with Lisa's name on it on the dining room table and plopped on the couch, calling for her.

"I'm in the shower; be right out." The bathroom door was open, but I had no desire to see her naked, not lately.

Lisa emerged in a terrycloth robe she had bought from Elizabeth Arden. In her attempt to fill her time, she had started to go to very expensive spas and hair salons.

She looked at me. "My God, Bobby, you better get to bed. You are going to leave me with a fatherless child. You look terrible."

I didn't like it when she joked about my health, but I knew she did it out of nervousness, so I ignored her. My cardiologist had warned me that medicine can only do so much and the rest was up to me. But I couldn't help myself. Work seemed to be the answer to all my problems.

Lisa spotted the envelope. "What's this?"

"It's a cohabitation agreement. I spent some time with a lawyer, Bill Drexler. Really nice. Not your typical family lawyer shark. We've put together this paperwork. Remember saying you'd sign anything I put in front of you? Well, this is it."

"Is this really necessary, Bobby?"

I didn't answer her question. Instead I said, "You need to get independent legal advice. Inside the envelope are some very confidential papers concerning my business. I'm trusting that you will show them only to your lawyer. Okay?"

"Sure, but who do I bring this to?"

"I can't help you. I don't want to be involved in it. Maybe Nicole can help you."

"Right. Duh. She works in a legal office. I'll call her tomorrow." Lisa did not open the thick manila envelope.

###

The week went by, and I had no idea if she saw a lawyer. And I never asked. It was like that elephant in the room people always talk about. Since she was starting to look pregnant and I was so exhausted, our sex life was pretty lame. It seemed like we were miles apart just when we should be the closest.

I was unprepared for what happened when I entered William Drexler's office the following week. Lisa had finally told me she had seen a lawyer in Nicole's office, but that was all she said, and I did not ask any questions. When Drexler greeted me with a serious look on his face, I got nervous.

"Thanks for sending the bottle of wine over at Aqua Blue the other night," Drexler said after we sat down. "We greatly appreciated it."

"My pleasure, Bill. Now what's new?"

Bill gave me the shocking news with a poker face. Apparently he played golf with a senior partner at the firm in which Lisa's lawyer worked, and the partner had given that lawyer, Kara Gilford, a rave.

"Lisa won't sign the agreement as is."

I explained that she had promised to sign anything, but this meant nothing in the end. "The net of the lawyer's response to our agreement was basically that she had advised her client not to sign the agreement, reasoning it was just too far from what she feels would be awarded by the court."

"But Lisa assured me she would sign anything."

"Well, apparently that's not the case. And her lawyer is correct. If Lisa ever did apply for child support, based on your present income she would most probably be awarded a great deal more than what you've offered."

"That's crazy, Bill. What did you put down as a monthly payment?"

"Five thousand dollars."

"And she would be awarded more by the courts?"

"Much more. The figure is based on a percentage of your income. And to be frank, you make a lot of money. My advice is either you go back to the lawyer and Lisa with a much better offer, or you just drop this for now. Give the two of you a little time and then revisit this in a few months. The reality is that she's pregnant, so the only one who can really benefit from this agreement is you. If you don't want to cohabitate, then we can just deal with the child support obligation."

I felt strangled by the situation, and my rage at Lisa rose to a lump in my throat. Or was it another heart attack? I wasn't sure. My divorce had not been pretty, but back then there wasn't enough money involved for the family lawyers to get their noses into my business. I had to get out of there. I needed to think.

"Thanks Bill, let me digest this. I'll get back to you."

"Bobby, it's hard to have a cohabitation agreement or a prenup executed when she's pregnant or when you're already married. There's just no leverage. Were you thinking of marrying her?"

"I don't know. I'm a little shell-shocked right now. I don't know what to think."

What I didn't say—what I could not say—was how shocked I was that Lisa reneged on her promise. That was the worst—worse than the business about the money. I had been brought up to believe that when you give your word to someone you care about, you keep that word. It was nonnegotiable. Lisa had basically lied to me—apparently without a backward glance. If she could lie now, she could always lie, and it might be about anything. The ground beneath my feet felt shaky. It was as though before the agreement I had been walking along like everybody else, but now I realized the earth might move any which way while I walked in a different direction. Shaky ground. I had never felt this uncertain of my world before. I felt betrayed.

CHAPTER FIFTEEN

I poured myself a drink. The idea that Lisa had not signed the agreement had me fuming. It was midnight, and she wasn't home. Lisa never went out late at night. Actually, I was a bit worried. She was nearly seven months pregnant. A good-looking woman in a vulnerable spot could get in a lot of trouble in the city. I called her cell phone but was sent immediately to voice mail, so I hung up. Perhaps some TV would help. But all I could do was surf channels with images of Lisa going through my brain—her demonstrations of devotion, how she wanted to give me a family and "would sign anything I put in front of her." I could even picture where she was the night she'd said it. We had argued and then made up. Now I looked back on that scene and wondered. Did she love me? Or did she just want me in her trap?

One o'clock in the morning came and went. I tried to read a biography by Caro on Lyndon Johnson, but I could not concentrate.

In the kitchen, I took out the makings for a healthy mozzarella and tomato sandwich on sourdough bread and placed it on a plate to microwave. I heard the door open. A quick look at my watch told me it was two o'clock. I had left the office and come home early tonight to talk about the agreement—but I'd be damned if I'd discuss it this time of night.

In the foyer, Lisa waved to me. "Hi, honey, you still up?" She slurred the "s" in the word "still" and leaned against the wall.

Before she could walk away, I grabbed her arm and said, "Lisa, what are you doing? You're pregnant. How can you get drunk? You're not supposed to be drinking any alcohol."

"Oh, Bobby, it was just one night. It's not going to hurt the baby. I think it's only the first trimester you have to worry about."

"Oh, and where did you get your medical degree? I heard Dr. Moss tell you no alcohol. No, as in none. How can you be so irresponsible? Have you ever known anyone with fetal alcohol syndrome?"

She pulled away from me. "I can't handle this. I'm going to take a shower."

I went back to my sandwich as Lisa showered, and I began to think. Who could she have been with? Definitely not Nicole or Katie, because they would not have let her drink. My fury was rising ever higher on the Richter scale. What muck had I got myself into with this girl?

Lisa came into the living room in her robe, drying her hair. She looked me straight in the face, and she seemed to have sobered up a little.

"Who were you out with?" I asked.

"Nicole and a couple of her friends from the office. We had dinner and then went to Bloody Mary's. I can't stay home all the time, you know. You're never here."

Chapter Fifteen

Something clicked inside me, and I went into the bathroom, shut the door, and turned the water on. I knew the night manager at Bloody Mary's, a woman who used to work for me. I quickly retrieved the number from my cell phone and called her. "Hey, Nell, Bobby Lakeland here. I was wondering—was Lisa there at all tonight?"

"Yeah," said the manager, "she was here earlier with a girlfriend and two guys I'd never seen before—you know, suits. Is everything okay?"

"Yeah, oh wait, I hear the door opening. There she is now. Thanks, Nell."

Back in the living room, Lisa was eating yogurt, her usual nighttime snack. Obviously she was getting ready for bed.

"So who were the people with you and Nicole?"

"Just two secretaries from her office. Why? You jealous?" Lisa walked over and tried to put her arms around me, but I shrank away from her.

"You're a liar," I said. "I know that you were with two men, and I don't get why you would lie about it unless you have something to hide. Just like I don't understand what kind of game you're playing with the agreement I asked you to sign."

"Bobby, wait a minute…"

"Go to sleep, Lisa. We'll talk in the morning."

"No. I want to talk now."

"Do you have any idea how mad I am at you? I can't talk reasonably right now."

"No, you can't drop a bombshell on me and then say we'll talk about it in the morning."

"Lisa, you're pregnant, and you need to sleep." I was putting on my sport jacket.

"Where are you going?"

"Away from you."

"Well, don't bother. I'm going."

"Where do you think you're going? It's three in the morning, and you're not leaving this apartment."

"Oh, yes I am. You're not my boss, Mr. Control Freak. I'm going to Nicole's."

"No. It's bad enough you went drinking. Now go to sleep."

Lisa threw her wet towel at me and headed for the bathroom. "Fuck you, Bobby."

When she emerged, she was dressed and carrying a little suitcase. I recognized the mood. There was no point in stopping her. "I'm not going to Nicole's. I'm going to my parents'. And don't ever contact me again. You can take your agreement and your…"

"My what, Lisa, my money?"

"You bastard," she said, and she slammed the door.

Days went by, and I tried to work myself into forgetfulness. I couldn't help but wonder how Lisa was doing as we hadn't talked since the fight. I thought about calling her mother, but I decided against it. I had to let this business run its course for a while. Maybe I really was better off without Lisa. I kept playing all the events over and over in my mind. I wasn't sure, but I thought it was possible that the courts wouldn't be able to grab as much money from me for paternity support if we weren't living together. I just couldn't shake the thought that Lisa had betrayed me.

A month went by, and still there was no word from Lisa. Then a card came in the mail. I had almost forgotten it was my birthday. She had made the card herself. It was no work of art, but I was touched by the effort. It was a crude drawing of a baby and a teddy bear. For days I pondered how I should respond. Finally I broke down and talked to Dave about it.

Dave pretty much knew blow-by-blow what had gone down since the cohabitation agreement became an issue. We spent a couple of nights meeting for drinks and discussing women in general. Dave had fallen hard for the lawyer he met during the summer, and she had dumped him, so both of us had some healing to do. Nothing was better than commiserating with a friend.

I asked Dave to meet me at another bar near Aqua Blue for a drink. I was careful about where I went because I didn't want to run into Lisa or her posse. I had the bartender set us up with a Stella and a shot. We sat alone at one of the small tables in the bar area.

"I really don't know what to do," I said to Dave. "If I call her, I know it will start all over again. Not only because she wants it, but honestly I do too. I miss her. And I'm beginning to get really excited about having the baby, how much it will mean."

"You really sure?"

"No, of course not. But when I got that birthday card, something broke inside me, and I felt all my resistance fall. I do love Lisa, and I guess I got over being afraid of the baby in these past few weeks."

"Well, if you want the baby, that's important. I think you should concentrate on that aspect. That's huge, man."

"Yeah, I know."

Dave downed his shot in one gulp, and I signaled for another round. "Are you sure about all this?" Dave asked again.

"Like I said, no. I'm not sure. That's the problem."

"Okay, take her out, but limit it. Take her out for a cup of coffee and see how it goes. Start all over like it's a first date. Maybe you'll see her through different eyes. Who knows?"

I thought this might be a good place to start. The next morning, I called Lisa. Her mother answered the phone.

"Hello, Darlene, this is Bobby. Is Lisa there?" I didn't want to get into a discussion with her mother. God forbid.

"Yes, Bobby. Nice to hear your voice." The reception I got from her mother was telling.

A minute went by, and Lisa got on the phone.

"Hello?" I had forgotten how sweet her voice could sound when she wasn't angry.

"Hey, thanks for the card. You know, I forgot it was my birthday."

"Oh, no, you can't do that. Don't forget your birthday." I could tell from her pitch she was excited to get my phone call.

"Speaking of which, how are you feeling?"

"Great, actually. I have tons of energy. I've been sleeping a lot and going out with Mom."

There was a brief pause, and then we both started to speak. I let her talk. "Would you like to get together for a cup of tea?" she asked me.

"I was going to ask you the same."

"Well, then I guess it's the right thing to do."

"Tomorrow?"

"Sure, let's go to the café opposite Aqua Blue—I don't remember the name."

"Breads. Sure, I'll be there."

###

"You look great." It was the first thing I said when I saw her, and it was true. Her pregnancy was obvious, and she looked adorable. Her skin was fabulous.

"Thank you. So do you."

There wasn't much to say. Or rather, words weren't what it was about. Clearly, Lisa had done a lot of thinking, too. Over coffee and tea, we sorted out our feelings about everything on our minds, except for the agreement.

"Let's not talk about the agreement right now," I suggested.

"That's fine with me," Lisa said. "The whole idea creeps me out."

"Well, I felt totally betrayed that you promised to sign it and then pulled a switcheroo."

Lisa put her chin in her hand and thought for a moment. "Truly, I told the lawyer that I didn't think it was right, but she kind of bullied me."

"And then you lied about who you were with that last night. Why?"

Tears filled Lisa's eyes. "You bully me too sometimes, Bobby. And I get afraid, so I say the thing I think will wash. It's not right, but it's kind of your fault."

I was stunned by this. I had never thought of myself as a bully, but maybe I did make her nervous. After all, I was eighteen years older, and I forgot sometimes what it must be like for her at this stage of her life. I've been told that my presence has a natural aura of intimidation.

We talked over what had gone on since we had separated, and we realized it had been three weeks since we had spoken. Both of us had changed how we felt. Tears welled up in Lisa's eyes many times, and I held on to her hand on the table until it felt totally natural that I should be holding on to her.

Finally, I said, "Will you come home?"

"I'll come home if you promise never to kick me out."

"Lisa, I didn't kick you out. You left, remember?"

She bit her lip, a habit of hers when she was deliberating with herself. "Right, you got me there. Okay, so I need to pack. But I'd like to come home right now, if that's okay, and get my stuff tomorrow."

"Done," I said. Outside the restaurant, I held her in my arms. Her stomach was keeping us apart a bit, and I loved it. Now tears were filling my eyes. "I can't wait to have this baby, Lisa."

"I love you, Bobby. We'll be a great family."

###

Right on time, the baby was ready to be delivered on September 6. She was born by cesarean section at Beth Israel Hospital at nine o'clock in the morning—a very civilized birth, as Mrs. Babcock said. She didn't quite understand this new idea of doctors scheduling cesareans to make their lives easier, but the baby was gorgeous. I was with Lisa in the delivery room.

A couple of hours later, Lisa was still groggy, but her parents were in her hospital room, where the baby was cuddled in her arms. The room was filling with flowers and balloons as the word got out that the new Ms. Samantha Lakeland had arrived into the world. I went off into a corner and called my son to tell him he had a little sister.

"Great," the boy said, "now you'll probably give me even less attention than you already do."

This sent a jolt to my heart to mar a perfect day. But I promised myself I would not neglect my son. I would make more of an effort to be even closer to him now. Then I went back to see my daughter.

Section V: Release

CHAPTER SIXTEEN

I wanted Lisa and the baby out of the city even if it meant I had to commute. Every time a siren went off on the street, the baby cried. Lisa was not a natural as a mother—there was no getting around it. Any upset with the baby threw her into panic mode. The country, I kept thinking. Maybe a place with horses. Besides, Lisa needed something to do. She was pouty, not losing the baby fat, seeming a little depressed. The truth was that I was worried she'd start drinking, and that really worried me because she was nursing the baby. She needed a change.

When I spotted the horse farm for sale in Rhinebeck, everything clicked together. The three of us took a ride up to the little town on the Hudson and met the realtor, a nice woman named Amy. She sold us on the town first, an old river town that was now a high-end home to artists and businesspeople, a mix of second homes and people like me who commuted everyday on Amtrak. The trip into the city along the river was, Amy said, as beautiful as "a trip down the Rhine." The trains went to and from the city every hour.

Both of us fell in love with the town first. In the center of the town is a grand old inn called The Beekman Arms, built a century ago out of stone. It's a landmark inn, a magnet for visitors from all over the world like the old Saratoga Springs hotels. The homes near town are big, old-fashioned farmhouses. But Lisa and I wanted space.

Amy had saved the best for last, of course—a twenty-acre former working farm. The owner had died, and the family had not kept the farm going or put the farm up for sale. It had been empty for a year. What happens when a house is left lonely showed that the house needed work. We walked the grounds surrounding the house. I was holding my gorgeous daughter, who was three months old, in a halter around my chest, and her little face leaned against my shoulder. Once in a while she moved her head around to see what was going on around her.

It was a gorgeous day, a crisp, clear December day with the sun shining and hardly any wind. I tried to imagine the house in the freezing winter, but it was too beautiful outside. Anyway, it hardly mattered. Lisa was obviously in love with the place. I was sure she had horses rather than sugar plums dancing in her head. We went back to the real estate office and took a virtual tour of the rest of the grounds. I put a binder on the property, figuring we could put the condo up for sale. Things happened really fast after that. The apartment was sold for the asking price by a couple I was certain would pass the board, and they paid cash. It seemed a signal from somewhere that we were supposed to buy the farm. That was that. I was going to be a commuter living on a hobby farm. The theme song from the old TV show *Green Acres* started playing in my head.

I have to hand it to Lisa—she had a burst of energy, considering the baby was only six months old. She wanted everything, and she wanted it immediately. That meant we had huge crews of laborers around us just about all the time. It was easy to get artisans—that was the other thing about Rhinebeck and the surrounding areas. The woodworkers, carpenters, floor people, barn builders—everyone had incredible talent, and they were pricey. By the spring, we had redone the old farm kitchen entirely. I have to say this was at my insistence, and we did it right out of *Architectural Digest*. The rest of the interior needed repainting and refurbishing.

Then there were the furnishings, tile, carpeting, and all the decorations. I have to admit that this part was a lot of fun. Fixing up an old farm was a labor of love for me. Lisa and I both enjoyed seeing all the renovations take place on a daily basis. Money was going out faster than I thought it would. But the end result was spectacular. Lisa oversaw the barn renovations, complete with new stalls, a tack room, and feed room. There were paddocks built, run-in sheds, and some farm machinery was purchased.

The commuting was not a piece of cake, but it was worth the sacrifice. I found the hour commute to be a welcome routine, and I loved coming home to the farm.

I don't want to forget O'Brien in all of this because, of course, O'Brien moved in with us as soon as the barn was ready. I bet the stable was sorry to see that income stream shut down. Lisa mucked the stalls and fed him and the other farm critters prior to me leaving for work in the morning. The stable grew from a few stalls into an established complex.

Lisa was ready to take the next step. To her credit, she had met a bunch of neighborhood moms with children of similar ages. It was Lisa who was instrumental in organizing them for gatherings. Our place was the favorite for many a get-together. I was glad to see her making new friends and becoming a member of the community.

But she was bored, and she wanted to do something with the horse farm. In the vicinity, there was an advertised horse and tack auction that we went to one Tuesday evening. This was my first exposure to this kind of an event. I had been to auctions before, but never a horse auction. What a hoot!

There were tons of country folk looking over the horses housed in makeshift stalls prior to the actual bidding. In a riding ring, you could ask to see the horse under saddle for those who knew what to look for. I love the snack bar foods of grilled burgers, freshly cut fries, peanut brittle, and the smell of freshly roasted coffee.

We thoroughly enjoyed it, and I asked Lisa all kinds of questions about the different kinds of horses, why people would buy them, sell them, and so forth. Samantha was the hit of the auction, and I was so proud to show off my six-month-old sweetheart.

One of the horses that Lisa had her eye on was a good-looking bay. As we watched it in the auction corral, Lisa said, "I bet I could make a profit on that horse."

Hearing the word profit got my attention, and I asked her what she meant.

"Bobby, imagine taking this horse, cleaning her up, and putting her on the farm, how beautiful she would look. She would make a young girl a great hunter or jumper."

"How would you advertise it?"

"I would put an ad on the Internet."

"How much do you think you could sell her for?" I asked.

"I don't know, maybe four or five thousand. Let's see what she sells for."

Lisa and I were curious to see the results as the bidding commenced. The professional and folksy auctioneer started the bidding at five hundred dollars. Hands went up, and after a few more rhythmic verses of his auction mantra, I made out that the bidding had risen to a thousand dollars. Things started to slow down at thirteen hundred.

Lisa said, "Bobby that's unbelievable—what a steal at thirteen hundred."

We next heard, "Going once, going twice…sold, for thirteen hundred dollars."

On the way back from the auction, Lisa was going a mile a minute, talking about that bay. I could tell she was really excited. We had found out that this auction was held every second Tuesday evening.

I said to Lisa, "Why don't you show me the horse classifieds on the Internet after we put Samantha to bed."

The next morning, Lisa asked what I thought of the auction, and she went on to say, "Bobby, I was thinking. What if I went to the auction in two weeks and bought a horse? I'll clean it up, give it some nutritious food, put some weight on it, ride it and do some work with it, and then advertise it on the Internet and sell it. What do you think?"

Secretly, I was ecstatic. I loved the fact that she came up with the idea, and it would be a venue for her to start a business, albeit small, but still a business. She could do it on her time around the needs of Samantha and the neighborhood get-togethers. I asked her how this would affect Samantha—who would take care of her when she was showing horses or working with them, and how she would have the time to do the extra work required.

Lisa promised that this would in no way affect Samantha. She was giving riding lessons to one of the neighbor's teenage daughters, and in lieu of money, she was willing to trade for babysitting.

I asked her what would happen if she couldn't sell the horse. Her response was a good one. "I'll just put it back in the auction."

I smiled at her, proud of her answer.

"Bobby, will you lend me the start-up money to buy my first one, transport it, buy extra feed, have the vet come and give it what it needs, and advertise it, get business cards, and so on? I don't need that much—let's say five thousand dollars? I'll pay it back as soon as I can from the profits."

I said okay. She got off her chair and hugged me. She was so excited. I, in turn, was excited as well.

"You'll see, Bobby. I'm going to do this all by myself and run it like a real business, keep the books, and make a profit."

As I was commuting to Manhattan on the train, I reviewed the business formula of Lisa's new venture. Take a horse at an auction that looks disheveled, buy low, take it to our beautiful property, clean it up, give it what it was lacking, take a photo of the horse grazing in our paddock, advertise it, have people come to our property and ride it, and then sell it for a profit. I smiled, remembering Lisa's words: "I'm going to do this as a real business all by myself." I was proud of her. This was a good fit with very minimal downside.

Every second Tuesday, Lisa, Samantha, and I went to the horse auction. It became a routine outing that I enjoyed. Lisa budgeted one horse to buy. Her top price she would pay would be twenty-five hundred dollars. I would hold Samantha while she went to see the horses, checked for proper health concerns, and examined their legs. Often, she rode one prior to the auction to see how the horse handled. She took this very seriously as she was looking for the right horse with hunter or jumper potential.

One particular auction evening, Lisa bought her horse and was arranging for transportation back to the farm. Another horse entered the auction corral that Lisa hadn't seen before. It was a big, black Percheron. The gelding was under saddle and being ridden in the ring. Lisa's eyes were glued to this horse.

"Oh, Bobby, I know someone who is looking for exactly this horse. I can make a quick sale like in two days."

I asked, "How much can you make?"

She said, "I can get about four thousand. Can you lend me the money so I can buy him?"

I nodded in the affirmative. Lisa bought the big boy for eighteen hundred dollars. There were three others bidding, but Lisa got him. True to her word, Hercules—that was the name she gave him—was sold for forty-five hundred dollars on Friday. She sold him to a woman in the Catskills who was looking for a big horse. I thought to myself that after Lisa paid me back and after expenses, she would make twenty-five hundred dollars in three days! Here was the problem: Lisa never wrote me the check for the eighteen hundred dollars I advanced her. I didn't say anything, figuring she would get around to it. I was mistaken.

Time passed. Lisa turned out to be a natural at her business. I marveled at how good she was at closing the deal. I knew if she could get them to the farm, she had a good chance of making the sale. Pretty much all of the purchasers were women, and Lisa befriended them. Once again, I secretly admired her ability. Lisa was becoming very confident and independent. In addition to the local auction, we were attending other auctions out of town to find more inventory. She now had two neighbors taking lessons, and both traded her for babysitting Samantha, who was now fifteen months.

One day when I got to my office, I started to feel woozy. Ever since my heart attack I was more attuned to my body, if not more careful about my health. There was a bug going around, and I did not want to get sick and endanger the baby, so I decided to knock off early and work from home.

Lisa's SUV was parked at the barn when I arrived home, so I drove up there. What I found was my daughter strapped to her car seat in the backseat with the windows open, crying and screaming at the top of her little lungs. I took my daughter out of the car seat. Large, green horseflies buzzed around her face. She needed her diaper changed. I thought about the stages of development and just how much trauma might accrue from this incident to a fifteen-month-old child. I wanted to punish Lisa. I wanted her to feel as frightened and abandoned as Samantha was feeling.

I checked the stable and saw that two horses were out. My brain could not take it in. What was this woman thinking, leaving an infant alone, exposed? I lost all respect for her. She was a self-indulgent, spoiled child who could not think straight or make adult decisions, and she was playing house at my expense. She was using my money, she was using me, but worst of all, she was endangering my little girl.

Back at the house, I changed the baby, gave her juice, and realized that she was thirsty and hungry. This time the thought of leaving Lisa was conscious, not subconscious. Not only was I going to dump her, I was going to leave her hungry, just like my daughter. Then it hit me. We had never signed a cohabitation agreement.

Dinner that evening was predictably all my favorite foods. Lisa was dressed in the baby-doll dress she knew I liked with ballet shoes. The Joy perfume I had purchased for her would have been intoxicating, but to me it smelled like all the things that go along with deception. In essence, she was the snake in the Garden of Eden.

Once we were seated with the candles lit, she said, "Bobby, I am so sorry. I don't know what I was thinking. I just never thought you'd come home in the middle of the day."

"So you're sorry you got caught? How often has my daughter been left in her car seat alone?"

Lisa started to answer, but I didn't let her finish. It would only be a lie. "Don't answer. I won't believe a word you say. Just tell me this—didn't you think for a minute that someone might have seen you leave the baby alone and kidnap her? Do you know that predators like little babies—like to steal them for money? Some like to steal them for sex?" At this she had the decency to wince. "Do you have any idea how frightened she was? How long do you think it will take for her to recover from being abandoned like that? Have you read any of the parenting books I've brought home?"

Lisa again tried to talk, but I was not letting her get a word in. I was, I have to admit, somewhat out of my mind with horror at how irresponsible this woman/child was, this woman who was living a charmed life.

"You did the most irresponsible thing a parent can do. If a neighbor called child protection services, they would have come and taken the baby away. Do you realize that?"

Incredibly, her response, and I remember it verbatim, was, "I knew you were going to flip out. That's just

like you, Bobby. Mr. Boss Man. I'm not one of your employees. You can't scold or fire me. If you would have
hired that full-time nanny I liked from the Philippines,
this would not have happened."

It was so like Lisa, to blame everyone else.

And that's what I said to her.

She threw a Pepsi can at my head and ran from the
table into the bedroom.

I heard the baby crying. That grounded me. *Oh, my
God, what am I going to do?* I thought.

CHAPTER SEVENTEEN

Lisa began to complain about money. I explained a number of times that her money was tied up in inventory. By this point she had nineteen horses on the property, and when I suggested she sell them, she claimed it was not a good time. I didn't know enough to question her. What did she need the money for? More equipment and feed? Money to pay the trainer she had hired? I patiently explained that she was using the household resources to pay for the stable at this point, and it was not good business. She should let the stable be independent by selling some of the horses to put money into the stable.

"You're so controlling." This was her favorite and usually her first strike. I sometimes thought I should block Dr. Phil from our cable. But the last time she asked for money, I reminded her that she had wanted to be independent, which was admirable, but the only way to do so was to keep her business cash flow separate from our household finances.

"I'll go over the finances with you. I'd be happy to."

"No thanks," I remember her saying. "I'll get the money somewhere else. Thanks for nothing."

Thanks for nothing. I wanted to throttle her. We lived in a town that ran alongside the Hudson River.

Outside her window was twenty acres of first-rate property, some of it meadow, some woods. All of this led to her stable. There was a bridle path that ran through the woods, across a running stream, and to a field where the horses could gallop around to show their stuff to prospective buyers. She had a bright, gorgeous child. If this was nothing, then there was something missing inside Lisa. I felt sorry for her, really. But it was time for this woman/child to grow up and take on responsibility.

I was in my office reviewing my personal bank statements—a task I disliked enough to attack quarterly rather than every month. To my horror, there were withdrawals that were not mine. It was my habit to withdraw two hundred and fifty dollars at a time to know that the withdrawals were mine. The month I was reviewing had erratic sums withdrawn. I immediately called my bookkeeper, Ricky, into my office, simultaneously calling the bank and canceling the card. Ricky and I went over the last three months and estimated there were ten thousand dollars in strange withdrawals. The sensation of my stomach rising to meet my whirligiging brain was familiar to me; it was confusion and fear. Yes, I was controlling when it came to not knowing who was invading my bank account.

The bank was one block away, and we ran there—no coats, just whatever we wore in the office. We found the police waiting for us because the bank manager had called them. Once seated in a conference room, the older of two uniformed cops asked me if anyone else knew my password.

"My partner."

"Business partner?"

"No, I mean my domestic partner."

"Did she withdraw the money?"

Good point. I banged her speed dial number into my cell phone and told her what happened. Her shock was apparently sincere. Who could have done such a thing, and how could they have gotten the password? "What's the password?" she asked, though I was certain she knew it was the same as my computer password and last four digits of my Social Security number. I had told her this in case something happened to me and she needed to get her hands on the money.

I told her I had to get back to the police and that I would see her and the baby later. When I turned my attention back to the meeting, the lead cop told me he would turn the information over to the detective in the precinct who specialized in bank fraud and to expect to hear something in about two weeks. Meanwhile, the bank hurried to set me up with a new account. The ten thousand was history. It hurt.

Two weeks later, a Detective Ward called me. "Do you want to do this in person or over the phone?" he said.

"Do you have an answer for me?" I asked.

"I do."

"Let's spare each other some time. What have you learned?"

"Well, Mr. Lakeland, I hate to tell you this, but the person withdrawing the money is Lisa Babcock, who I understand is your domestic partner and has denied withdrawing the money. Is that true?"

I must have answered an assent, but I don't recall. My first instinct was to cover my ears like a five-year-old and scream so I did not have to hear the truth. The betrayal was shattering. In fact, I could not believe it.

"How do you know this?"

"Each transaction is linked to a particular machine. The machine has a camera that takes an image of each person withdrawing funds. I went to your home today and met Lisa. I told her that we had the evidence that she had made the withdrawals, and she admitted it was true. I'm sorry, but unless you want to press charges, this seems like a domestic problem."

I don't know what I said. He wished me luck. I sat down in my desk chair. The feeling of betrayal had turned into disgust. What was worse? Her being with another man or stealing money? Someone walked in my office, turned around, and walked out. This was enough to make me realize I had to get out of the office to think.

CHAPTER EIGHTEEN

What kind of people brought up a daughter who snuck money from her partner's bank account? Basically, the Babcocks were good people. This action on Lisa's part must be aberrant. I decided to ask Lisa's father for help.

Ernie,

I struggled with the most appropriate way to communicate the following to you. I chose an e-mail as the best way to tell you that Lisa has stolen more than $10,000 from me.

I was informed by a detective in the fraud department that Lisa has been withdrawing funds from my account via bank machines. He got an admission from her. He asked me what I wanted him to do.

I haven't spoken to her about this yet. I wanted to let you know as you might be able to shed some light on this. I don't know what I'm going to do.

Bobby

A short while later, I received the following:

Bobby,

Let me get to the bottom of this. Don't do anything rash in the meantime.

Ernie

I wanted to take a drive and think. I headed up the FDR toward Route 17 and was headed towards Poughkeepsie. I couldn't believe she had taken more than ten thousand in a three-month period. I started doing the math. Nineteen horses were fifteen more than usual. Three months was ninety days at $2.50 a day per horse in feed, which was $37.50 a day. I rounded that to forty a day times ninety days, which was only thirty-six hundred. Where did the other sixty-four hundred go? What else was she doing?

The reality was that if she was capable of stealing from me, she was capable of all kinds of infidelity. I thought back to Lisa leaving Samantha alone in the car, and I felt a surge of anger build up in me. Inside I was livid. What kind of a sucker did she take me for?

I decided to make an appointment with my lawyer.

My mind drifted back to my divorce proceedings in my first marriage, and I remembered the black cloud that followed me for the entire time period. A combination of fear and anxiety came over me. I realized this was much more than I could handle by myself. I needed help on this one. I think that's why I impulsively e-mailed Ernie. Perhaps a family intervention could force Lisa to see what she'd done and the harm it caused. We could get Lisa's family and her two friends and have an intervention where she could see that those who cared for her the most condemned her actions but still supported her. Yes! An intervention! I started to feel better knowing there was at least a plan of action. I would await Ernie's response. But Ernie never responded. His silence spoke volumes.

###

That evening I was ready to talk to Lisa. I read Samantha a story from a children's book, *The Little Engine That Could*, even though I was pretty sure she could not understand it. It made me feel strong. Samantha was asleep, her little backside in the air, by the fourth page of the book. I covered her and turned off the light. The tinkling carousel mobile above her head moved in the breeze created by the subtle movements. It struck me then that I could not leave Lisa because that would mean leaving Samantha. What a mess she had made of things.

Lisa was in the bedroom, seated at the mirrored and skirted authentic Chippendale vanity table we had bought from an antique store in Hudson. She had one foot up on the table, giving herself a pedicure. When I entered the room, she smiled seductively at me, but I did not even look at her. Instead, I sat on the corner of the bed closest to her and began to talk.

"Do you know what your behavior did to our relationship? You have broken our trust."

"Bobby," she said, putting her foot, half polished, on the carpeted floor. "What did you want me to do, let my horses starve? I asked you for the money, and you refused. It's your fault I had to steal."

"I suggested you sell a few horses to manage your cash flow. I offered help that way, but you insisted you do things on your own. As soon as things got tough, you cheated, Lisa."

She pushed her agenda. "All you had to do was lend me some money. I could have gotten through the winter and sold the horses when I could get a better profit. You have so much money; I don't see why you can't share it."

"Lisa, remember when I lent you eighteen hundred dollars to buy the Percheron and you got forty-five hundred in three days?"

"Yeah."

"You never paid me back."

"Eighteen hundred is nothing to you."

"Your word is something to me. That was broken, and that was when I decided not to lend you more money. Having nineteen horses is inventory. You have a hundred thousand dollars in the barn and in the paddocks now. You had the wherewithal to take care of your business on your own, as you say you want to do, and yet you stole my money."

"I did not steal your money. I am your domestic partner."

I was livid. I could not get through to her. She was a spoiled brat who wouldn't hear anything other than her own agenda's mantra. "Lisa, you need counseling. I think you are in denial about a lot of things, and I am not capable of fixing you."

Back in Bill Drexler's office, I felt a sense of "been there, done that." As I recounted the scenario to Drexler, I became even more disturbed by Lisa's actions. What kind of person was I living with?

"So," Drexler said, "do you want to leave her?"

"I can't handle her; she's out of control. But I don't want to lose my daughter the way I lost my son."

"You're getting ahead of yourself. Do you want to stay with Lisa, or is it too broken a relationship to try and put things back together?"

"What are you getting at, Bill?"

In answer, Drexler handed me a card from inside his desk. "This man is a marriage counselor. I've recommended him to a number of clients, and he's very insightful. He's a little out of the box, so to speak. He has a different way of dealing with things than other counselors. If nothing else, I think he can help you make a decision about the relationship. As far as custody goes, you've been down this path before. You know it's a very steep hill for you to get custody. It's possible, but it's a steep uphill battle. You know how courts are when it comes to custody matters. I would advise against it."

I really didn't want to break up another family and go through another broken life. I hoped this man could help. "Thanks, Bill."

CHAPTER NINETEEN

The trip to Isaiah Duncan's office was a trip indeed. I had not ever visited Queens except to pass through on the way to one of the airports. At one time parts of the borough had been upscale, Forest Hills Gardens was probably still protected behind its brick gates, but the rest of Forest Hills was an exurban motley cornucopia of strip malls and people. Buses battled with cars to find space around double-parked vehicles. Subway stops spilled hordes onto the streets. The difference between the poor and middle-class neighborhoods could only be differentiated by a certain feel—either one felt threatened or not.

Dr. Duncan's office was in Forest Hills Gardens on Burns Street, a few blocks south of the famous Tennis Club. I pulled the car in front of a classic nineteenth-century red brick building with huge wooden doors where a doorman stood at the ready. I could see that Lisa was very nervous, actually shaking.

"Don't worry so much. This man can help us."

"I don't like shrinks."

"He's supposed to be different."

"Where did you get his name?"

"From Dr. Gleason." I did not want her to know I had seen my lawyer, so I told her I had confided in the cardiologist that there was stress at home.

We emerged from the elegant, roomy old wood and brass elevator and turned to apartment 4B. The door was open. The waiting room had a white noise machine, silk-striped upholstered French chairs, and a couch. There was a piece of art on the wall of a man crossing a tightrope over the city. How very Freudian.

Before we could sit, a huge man in his early forties opened the office door. And I mean he was huge. This six-foot-seven man was not what I pictured as a marriage counselor. He looked like a pro football player. He must have weighed three hundred and fifty pounds. Isaiah pushed his hand out to shake Lisa's first, and her hand disappeared into his like a baby's into a giant's in a fairy tale. Black on white. Gently he greeted her and then turned to me and gave me the same greeting. Then we were all seated in his office.

"Lighten up, you two—this doesn't hurt."

I pointed to a picture of Isaiah on the wall. "You were a football player."

"Not pro. Just college. Let's talk about you." He proceeded to explain the process.

Lisa started. She went through her complaints about my controlling nature, especially when it came to money. She fessed up to the ten-thousand-dollar "loan," as she called it, and explained that her horses were going to starve because I would not give her the money even though I was filthy rich. Lisa went on for thirty minutes, running at the mouth and basically saying the same thing. Duncan turned to me and said, "Okay, your turn."

Lisa began to cry. The counselor handed her a tissue but did not stop the process.

I had taken notes as she spoke. I summarized exactly why we were there in "macro" terms and what I hoped to achieve. It took me three minutes.

Dr. Duncan said, "Okay. That's it for today. I want you to prepare the following for our next appointment, which will be the same time next week. I want you to write out in as much detail as possible how each of you would like to see your life three years from now. I mean each one of you writes it alone. That's it."

He walked us to the door. His size seemed less intimidating. I felt better. At least we were doing something about our problem.

Lisa and I were spending more time in the city. Between applying for kindergarten for Samantha and sessions with Dr. Duncan, it was too complicated for Lisa to travel back and forth with the baby. She hired two of her riding students to care for the horses and stable and kept her appointments to show the horses to weekends. As far as I could see, she was still keeping up her cash flow. I had not yet seen a penny of the ten thousand dollars, nor had she offered to pay me back. I seethed.

Our appointment at the Horace Mann Academy was heartening. The school, located in Riverdale, was one of New York's elite private schools. The student body included children of Fortune 500 executives, international diplomats, and Hollywood celebrities. There were underprivileged kids there on scholarship. I felt the mix was perfect for Samantha, who would be five next year and ready for school. It would be a thirty- to forty-minute drive for Lisa and Samantha, but we felt it was well worth the commute.

Our meeting with the headmaster, Mr. Kitchet, and the senior kindergarten teacher was brief but fruitful. As my child played in the corner with toys, we talked with the faculty. I tried not to dominate Lisa, but I diplomatically led our part of the conversation. Covering for Lisa's deficiencies was tiring, but I was determined that Samantha get into an excellent school.

Once back in the car, I commented that I hoped Samantha would get into the school. My own childhood public-school education left a lot to be desired and proved an obstacle when I got to college.

But I didn't want us to put too much pressure on the situation. "If they don't accept her, she'll be just fine…"

I remember the look on Lisa's face, a kind of snarl. "What do you mean, if they don't accept her? No public school for my baby. My little girl is going to have all the things I never had."

I pointed out that there were other private schools. But Lisa was responding to the possibility that anyone might reject Samantha. What I realized was that to Lisa, Samantha was just an extension of herself.

###

The second session with Dr. Duncan was revelatory. The doctor was not looking so much like a giant this time, more like a doctor as he sat behind his desk. He first asked if anything was new. When neither of us had anything to say, he turned to me and suggested we start with my list of what I would like my life to be in three years. I had prepared, as I always do, with notes, which I handed to him.

But Isaiah was having none of that. "Read them aloud."

I couldn't believe how nervous I felt. Here I was with only Lisa and the therapist to listen, but I broke into a sweat. I took a drink of water from the bottle I had brought in with me and began. I talked about the improvements I would make on our property, the planting of a vegetable garden, and my hope to make part of the farm yield something environmentally useful. I envisioned building an educational jungle gym for Samantha and imagined playing with her there. I knew Lisa was looking for a pony for Sam, and I saw myself walking her pony on a lead. I yearned for the time to sit outside the paddock and watch Lisa show off the horses. Also I was determined to create more time to just sit in front of the fire with my child and read children's books or books I had always meant to read, and I wanted time to listen to music on the sound system I had spent a fortune to install. Reading the list made me hungry to live this life.

Duncan smiled and turned to Lisa.

She had no list but said it was all in her head. Lisa did not see our property in her future. Instead, she described an entirely different piece of land and a very modern house. This total rejection was just one more blow I had to sustain. The feeling was getting routine. She described the Cadillac Escalade hybrid she would drive to and from her modern house to her heated stable. Her Prada and Dolce & Gabana outfits plus I. Miller riding outfits were covered along with the names of the friends she would make. We would donate thousands of dollars at charity benefits, and for these she would need more clothes. And travel. Lisa was heading straight for the Spanish Riding Academy in Austria to see the Lipizzaner. After that it was every hot spot from Central America, to Paris, to Buenos Aires, to Sydney, to Saint Bart's, and the Galapagos Islands. Certainly I would never be able to keep up. So I don't know who she was traveling with.

Isaiah must have seen the expression on my face because he turned to me and said, "Can you tell Lisa what you need? What you want?"

I started out with trust, that I needed to believe in her. Typically she cut right in, saying it was not her fault that I was so controlling that she had to go behind my back to get anything done. Lisa's reality was that nothing was ever her problem. Dry ice inside me burned until I pulled away some more. Isaiah reminded her that one of the rules we had agreed to was that we would not interrupt each other. He encouraged me to continue, while Lisa folded her hands in her lap and looked away—not contrite, just gone.

"I'm still so hurt about you taking money out of my account without asking. To me, this is just as bad as you being with another guy," I said "How can I trust Lisa again after this?" I posed this question to the room in general, to Isaiah and Lisa. "Lisa, you don't know how important this is for me."

That was her cue to run out of the office. The doctor and I sat there looking at each other for a moment. We did not bother to make another appointment. I paid him and left.

In the car, Lisa was seated in the passenger seat, still with that look of staring into someplace that I could not see. When I sat in the car without engaging the ignition, she said, "Aren't you going to start the car?"

I tried again to talk to her, asking how she could walk out of the session while I was pouring my heart out to her. "And your response is to ask if I'm going to start the car?"

"Bobby, get over it," was what she said. "You're just going to have to get past this. I said I was sorry. I shouldn't have done it, but I had no choice. I couldn't let my horses starve."

She was sticking to her story. The hell with me.

We did not go back together to Dr. Duncan. Lisa decided that Isaiah hated her and thought she was a terrible person. So I went to a session on my own.

Duncan put it to me forcefully. "You need to make a decision. Can you forgive her? What would you do if a few years from now you found Samantha going in your wallet and taking twenty dollars? Would you forgive her? Would you disown her and cut off your relationship with her?"

That got to me. Of course I would forgive Samantha.

CHAPTER TWENTY

Samantha loved school. More to the point, Lisa loved the whole milieu. For a while we were, if not happy, at least getting along. Samantha was a delightful child, bubbly and smiling. I lived to keep her happy. Lisa was a dutiful mother, never repeating the mistake of being irresponsible, so far as I knew. Lisa brought Samantha to school, but it became obvious that it was harder to set up playdates due to the distance.

As Samantha entered a new stage in her development, it was Lisa who really started to change. She was very social with the other parents at Horace Mann. Lisa started to go for coffee with the moms after dropping off their children, and there was a whole schedule of playdates and activities after school. Lisa got involved, and she began to serve on committees. Fundraising was her favorite, and there she was beginning to fulfill her dream. Horace Mann, like most private schools, raised money in many ways, and one was to hold an annual event that included a silent auction. Lisa was on the committee that went after the auction items.

The other committee mothers loved her. She was young in comparison to them because kindergarten mothers tended to have other young children and were too overscheduled to serve on these committees.

I saw this as a sign of maturity. She'd come home with talk of what she had managed to get donated—first editions of important books from a child's author parent; artwork; an hour of an exclusive lawyer's time; even lunch with a famous screenwriter at which the auction winner was invited to question the writer about tips on how to write a screenplay. She had wrangled about a hundred thousand dollars worth of product, and it was four months until the auction.

Of course the horses were taking a backseat, and Lisa was down to four. Truthfully, these were her personal horses. I was happy with what was going on at the property and realized that I, too, was fulfilling the dreams I had mentioned at the session with Dr. Duncan. I had built a trout farm and was delighting in a small operation of smoked trout called Sam's Smokes. Small restaurants and upscale markets were buying the product, distributed by a food rep. I also, of course, served the trout in my restaurants, and many times customers asked to buy the product, so all of the restaurants also sold it. The packaging had been designed by an artist in Rhinebeck. The whole operation was a work of the heart.

But Lisa was enthralled with the private-school scene. She loved dressing Samantha in children's couture, even to go on playdates. Once a week Lisa met for lunch with a group of mothers, and as time went on she became a completely different woman superficially. Her demeanor, hobbies, and points of references all became those of a woman who could never be mistaken for a former waitress. God only knows what background she made up for herself. Often during the week she attended charity events—the kind you read about in the society pages. Before the events there were parties for the women to have hair and makeup done. These were the evenings that Rochelle, the babysitter, took care of Sam, and I took care of business. Occasionally, Lisa dragged me along, which meant she talked me into an extremely expensive and uncomfortable tuxedo. But I found myself standing in the corner, observing my partner as she buzzed around, pollinating the scene and being pollinated. I prayed for patience and counted the hours until we could go home.

Ultimately, Lisa began to talk about that other property she had talked about in her plan for Dr. Duncan. Samantha's playmates all were moving to places like new gated communities.

I didn't know where she came up with Pleasure Valley. I was only familiar with the names of the people she associated with because I was careful who Sam was with. I knew there was Galton, the wife of a major league baseball player just moved up here from Atlanta. Mrs. Galton had a playdate at our house once, and I had the bad fortune to be home early that day. The nannies were with the children, making sundaes. The mothers were in the living room, drinking wine and gossiping. After greeting Nancy Galton, I hightailed it into the den. She was a very scary young woman, covered in diamonds and wearing jeans and stiletto heels.

Everything she owned looked untouchable. I knew there was a widow of a former Exxon executive who had been left a ton of money.

The "mom" I did not know about, because Lisa was cagey as always, was Simon Johnson. Mr. Johnson did not have to take his twin girls to school, but he had a lot of time on his hands. He was at that stage of wealth where he just let his money make money, while his much younger wife was busy planning and building her dream home. Mr. Johnson owned racehorses. By the time I found out about his presence on the ladies who lunched scene, Lisa had already ridden some of his horses with his trainers.

Lisa was too smart to immediately talk about Pleasure Valley. She first talked about this and that playmate who was moving out of the city. One was moving to the coast, another to the west coast of Florida. Certainly we would never leave New York. Canny as she was, Lisa mentioned another family from Horace Mann that was moving to Switzerland so their child could go to school there. Then she started talking about Chatham, a great place for kids to grow up, but too far really to commute. "How about Pleasure Valley?" she finally asked.

At this point, I don't remember even agreeing to move. I adored our farm. The sunset over the paddock as the horses grazed moved me. Each time I passed over the George Washington Bridge, I felt a sense of serenity fill me up and push away disorder and disease. "But we can just look," Lisa said.

Lisa's point was that now that Samantha was at Horace Mann, she was missing out on friendships and a normal childhood because of living so far away from her classmates. "Wouldn't it be great for her to have all her friends right there? A farm is so isolated for her. She is so alone here with no one to play with." Once again, it came down to Samantha. I thought of my own childhood and the fond memories of playing road hockey, baseball, and football in the street. I could see the benefit of Samantha living in a community and having friends/playmates on the street. I thought about it, and even though I loved the property and knew that Lisa's motivation was not thinking solely of Samantha's needs, I was thinking of Samantha. Some of her classmates' families were moving to a gated community near Pleasure Valley.

There were only a few homes left. The obvious last-choice homes were the least favorite for a variety of reasons. I was not impressed. I found the homes to be very pricey for what they were. When compared to our restored farmhouse, they were all such a letdown.

As we walked around the community, we did notice how many young children there were. We stopped by Samantha's playmate's house and received a warm welcome. They took us on a tour of the swimming pool, the fitness club, the golf club with its restaurants, board rooms, health club, tennis courts, playgrounds, and jogging tracks.

On the way back, we discussed the idea of moving. I asked Lisa about her horses. She said she could move them and that she wasn't interested in selling them anymore. She wanted to learn more about racehorses with the idea of training them.

"Where did this idea come from?" I asked.

"The father of one of Sam's classmate's races standardbreds. He's offered to take me as an apprentice. You remember Simon Johnson—we sat next to him and his wife Pauline at the silent auction."

This was a nice turn of events. Lisa had just spent the last two years building up her business. My estimate was that she must have made a hundred and fifty thousand dollars over the past two years. I never saw a penny of it and had no idea what she had done with it or where it was. All I knew was that for some reason she wanted to do an about-face and learn how to train standardbred trotters.

After giving it much thought, I decided that it really would be best for Samantha to live in a community. I wouldn't have my farm vistas, but at least I would know my child was growing up with lots of kids her age. I hoped that a move and a new environment just might be the trick for Lisa and me to heal our broken relationship.

CHAPTER TWENTY-ONE

We were happy, the three of us, for the first time in a long while. Lisa spent much of the first six months trying to decorate the new house. This space was totally different from the farmhouse, and she wanted a modern look. She was tired of the country style of our farm. She remodeled the entire first floor to turn it into a twenty-first-century steel and wood kitchen connected to a minimal dining room. She had the great room redone into an entertainment room with an area for the adults and an enclave for the children that included a miniature video arcade. I came home every day to carpenters, woodworkers, and wallpaper hangers, but Lisa had promised everyone bonuses to finish quickly, and soon the house was completed. Lisa was always generous with my money.

Sometimes I would come home unexpectedly and find Lisa away. Sam had a regular babysitter who accompanied her on playdates, even though she rode her bike within the community to her friends' homes. I knew that Lisa was trying to build a network within the community. The women played tennis at the country club, but Lisa did not play. Her horses were boarded at Simon's farm. Usually, Lisa arrived home in riding clothes, and I assumed she had been working out on her favorite, the first thoroughbred she purchased after Sam was born, a gray, dappled French warm blood named Rummy.

At the same time, Sam was making the leap from her Shetland to a Morgan, a small horse, but no longer a pony. She was taking riding lessons at Simon's. For no reason at all, this made me feel more comfortable about Sam's riding. It wasn't like Lisa could help Sam if something happened during a lesson, but she was there. Lisa was a yo-yo about most things in life, and truthfully she was more child than mother, but she was a first-class rider and certainly knew more about safety on a horse than any instructor.

For Sam's sixth birthday, we threw an extravagant party for twenty-five children, most of them Horace Mann students, and the rest of them children who lived in the neighborhood. All the parents were invited as well. We entertained the adults in the living room while the children were watched by their caretakers and entertained by a mélange of performers: a mime, which I had insisted on, and a sort of mobile petting zoo consisting of a llama pulled by a woman dressed like a Bedouin princess and a quite gymnastic monkey who jumped around on a jungle gym provided by his trainer. There was a cage of reptiles and crawly things on wheels to delight the boys. After the little pizzas and other comfort foods were served, a crew arrived and erected the trampoline I was surprising Sam with for her birthday. We had decided to serve the cake and ice cream after the trampoline to avoid sick tummies, which was a great idea. It was a huge hit, and I imagined that for many months to come, the children of Pleasure Valley would be showing up in our backyard.

I had not forgotten about Lisa's betrayal, but I had gotten past my rage. Reality was that if I wanted Sam in my life on a full-time basis, I had to have Lisa as well. Having been through one divorce, I wanted to have an intact family regardless of my feelings towards Lisa. One night when Sam had left the table, Lisa casually mentioned that Simon Johnson had offered her an opportunity to apprentice with his trainer at his horse farm. She went on to explain that she had to apprentice for two years to get her license.

Her casual delivery made me more suspicious than what she was saying. Nothing concerning horses for Lisa was casual, and she was apt to get into something and mistake the order of priorities. The horse farm was about twenty minutes away from the community, so that was not too much of a problem, but training trotters starts early in the morning, and of course, when the races are in season, they are at night. Lisa was not going to get paid for this training since she was an apprentice.

Lisa addressed my concern that she would be ducking her responsibility to Sam. She looked me dead in the eye and swore that nothing would come between her and her commitments at home.

I called Simon at his home and spoke to him about Lisa. "Simon, I understand from Lisa that you offered to have her apprentice with your trainer."

"Yes, she would work with him. In order for her to get her license, she would need to apprentice for two years. After that, she would take a written exam, and then she could get her New York State trainer's license."

"Is there a need for trainers?" I asked.

Simon laughed. "There's always a need for good ones. I'll tell you what I'll do. If Lisa gets her license, I'll give her one of my promising young two-year-olds to train. That will get her started. If she does well, I'll give her more and recommend her to others."

"That's very kind of you. What kind of time commitment is required of her during the apprenticeship?"

Simon replied, "Her time would be totally flexible. She can make her own hours, and it won't interfere with family time—that I can promise you."

"That's great, Simon. Do you think Lisa could be a standardbred trainer?" I asked.

"I believe she has a natural instinct with horses. She'll have to pick my trainer's brain and ask him lots of questions. If she puts the work in and doesn't mind the hard work, she could be very successful."

So it came to be. Lisa started her apprenticeship with Nick Gratton, a well-respected trainer of standardbreds. He had been training Simon's horses for years and had a solid reputation as a top-level trainer. Lisa sold off her remaining inventory of jumpers and hunters and was down to O'Brien, Rummy, the Shetland, and Samantha's new horse, Sir Galahad. Sam loved naming everything, and she had a real talent for it, too. When Simon mentioned that his wife, Pauline, had thought this was a great opportunity for Lisa, that kind of put my mind at ease about Lisa being around Simon's property all the time. After all, Pauline and Lisa were friends—or so I thought at the time.

CHAPTER TWENTY-TWO

Samantha turned eight the year Lisa's apprenticeship was over. It was also the period when I felt our relationship was deteriorating further. There is a reason such adages as "Monday morning quarterback" stand the test of time, and this one was certainly true for me. Only in retrospect did I see clues that I should have noticed that revealed Lisa's betrayal. Other betrayal. Or another betrayal. Whichever. The point is, Lisa had immediately broken her promise to keep her priorities straight and was soon letting other mothers pick Sam up at school, outsourcing her lunch to caterers, and leaving Sam at her mother's or sister's house on weekends if I was working. And then there were the bits and pieces that were even more glaring.

One morning Lisa had to go to work early, and I wondered how often the babysitter was the person who saw Sam off on the bus. I watched Lisa dress that morning and paid attention to the niggling voice that had been scratching for my attention: she was dressed to kill as she had been most mornings these days. No jeans and flannel shirt for this girl. I took a mental step back from Lisa and saw that she was hot; her camisole was peeking out from a denim shirt with lace-lined pockets right where her boobs poked out, and her jeans were so tight she could not have held a dime in the pocket. I think I knew right then that she was having an affair, but honestly, who wants to face facts all the time? So, I picked an argument about how little she was doing for Sam and around the house. This just made her more distant. There were now biweekly ladies' nights out, and when I found breath mints in her car, she explained that she used them to cover up the few cigarettes she smoked on these nights with the girls. I opened my mouth to confront her, but Sam was in the room, asking Lisa a question about her horse. By the time we were alone together, the moment had passed.

Every opportune moment passed. One day I got a call from Aqua Blue that two waitresses called in sick and the hostesses had to cover. In all the years we had been together, I had never asked her to come in to help at any of the restaurants, and now there were five. I reached her on her cell and asked if she could come in and help. She said she was needed at Simon's farm. When I said I would call Simon, she said flat out, "I don't think it's a good idea for us to work together." I hung up the phone and reflected. She had the audacity to say no to me and the business that supports her "apprenticeship" but gets up in the middle of the night to work with Simon's horses?

On it went. Sam kept growing closer to her mother, and I kept growing further away. Pleasure Valley was the perfect site for all of us, and this should have been utopia for us. Only Lisa was never there, and I was losing self-respect, perspective, and becoming emotionally bankrupt. If it weren't for my child, I would have been out of there.

Lisa started spending whole Saturdays or Sundays away at horse sales with Simon Johnson, his trainer, and the stable manager. Or that's what she said. I knew she was friendly with Simon's wife. Occasionally she asked me to accompany her on these trips, but I did not want Sam exposed to the racehorse world. It was nothing like show horses. Racing people were a different breed. They swore and cursed. They were horse thieves in the true sense of the word, dishonest by nature. So I stayed home with Sam. Lisa spent more time at the racehorse farm and the training track. She was now in the travois, working out the horses. She was in her element. She seemed to be putting more effort into her appearance. She was becoming a different person. Certainly she no longer needed me—other than the financial support I provided. I suppose that was good for her. I tried to be supportive, but the truth was I was not that happy about this new Lisa. I could feel her leaving us, me and Sam. Our sex life was nonexistent now. I was totally turned off.

One evening event, we ran into Simon and his wife, Pauline. As soon as the four of us coalesced into a group and I shook hands with Johnson, a vibration crawled up my spine, a frisson. I got a hold of it long enough to know that there was something in the air I was picking up on. I did not like Simon Johnson. Was that it? Lisa made small talk with Pauline, and her warmth and friendship with the other woman threw me off the notion that there could be anything but business between Lisa and Johnson. Still, I did not like the strange vibration.

It all came to a head when we were headed to a Christmas party for the parents of one of Sam's friends in Manhattan. We had not actually been alone with a good forty-five minutes ahead of us in months. The car was brimming with tense silence, nothing comfortable here. Lisa kept bringing the visor down to look in the mirror and fool with her hair and makeup and the Cartier diamond earrings I had purchased for her birthday. Finally when she could fool no more, she turned to me, and I can remember my shock. She said, "Well, I hope you are going to be friendly tonight. These are Samantha's friends. What's with you, anyway? Are there problems at work?"

I pulled the car over and put it in park. "No, Lisa, It's you. I'm disappointed in you. You promised the apprenticeship wouldn't interfere with us, me and Sam, but you are never home. I feel like I must be number eighty-three on your priority list. You won't lift a finger at home, but you'll muck out Simon Johnson's stalls."

"I don't muck out stalls. I'm a trainer. You are always belittling my career. I'm making money now."

"You're making ten dollars an hour and paying the babysitter twelve."

"So that's what this is about. Money. It always comes down to money with you. Money and control. You're getting nervous that you won't be able to control me when I get my training license."

I was pissed. Whenever we argued, Lisa fell back onto this control-freak thing. That was my vulnerable spot.

So I resorted to the button I could push in her. "You're piling a lot of stuff under the rug, don't you think? You might remember there is the incident of ten thousand dollars you took without asking that hangs between us. You never showed any remorse. It makes me worry, yes, about your motives. Do you blame me?"

"Bobby. Do you know how much money I could get from you in child support right now? But I'm still here. I stay with you because I love you. I've asked you to get past what happened. Isaiah asked you to get past it. I love you, baby, and I'm here."

She moved in for the close. "For me the big problem is that we never got married. I know how the other women look at me, what they must think, that if you really loved me you would marry me. How do you think that makes me feel?"

"We aren't married because you wouldn't even sign a cohabitation agreement."

"What about Samantha? She's getting to that age when her friends might start to tease her about the fact that her parents aren't married. That would devastate her."

Once again, Samantha's needs came to the forefront. The thought of her being called the "B" word was too much for me to fathom. I certainly wanted to prevent any emotional trauma that Samantha would have to face.

That evening while Lisa was being the social butterfly, I was weighing the pros and cons of marrying her. Bill Drexler had pointed out that because of the length of time that we had been living together, being married didn't really make that much of a difference other than property distribution. It wouldn't affect child and spousal support awards. I also thought, I'm stuck with her anyways as I wouldn't leave Samantha, and maybe being married might actually help the situation. (Always the eternal optimist, I guess.) As usual, I did the right thing for Samantha.

Three weeks, later we held a small wedding in our living room. A justice of the peace married us while our daughter, David Salzman, Nicole, Katie, and Lisa's parents looked on. My son had refused to come, which cast a shadow over the day for me, but Lisa looked beautiful in her Vera Wang slip dress and veil. My first wife and I were kids when we married and sort of hippies. This was a *Modern Bride* kind of small wedding with a sitdown lunch and a harpist. All the women cried, and the champagne was the best. I have to admit, it was pretty special. I'm not sure what Samantha understood. She stood next to Lisa in a velvet pink dress and Mary Janes, holding her mom's hand for most of the ceremony. My diamond girl. It was official. We were the Lakeland family.

The issue of the prenup, of course, never came up this time. We simply kept to the same routine as prior. I gave Lisa her weekly amount and never asked her what she spent it on. So when Lisa called to tell me a horse sale had come up in Binghamton, a two-hour drive away, and could she borrow some money to buy a standardbred of her own, I went into instant recall. What happened to the few horses Simon was supposed to be giving her to train? He did not have any available, Lisa replied. I forced myself not to go back even further to think about that wretched ten thousand dollars. I suggested we talk about it face-to-face.

I left the office and walked all the way uptown to the Seventy-ninth Street entrance into Central Park, a good five miles. I was caught up in spinning scenarios: If my dad were alive when I finished at Cornell, would he have lent me money to start a business? Would I have asked him? How ridiculous was that! It would not have occurred to me to ask anyone. Perhaps these days I might have applied for a small business grant. If Sam asked me someday for money to start a business, my answer would be the same. Exactly the same. Why should it be any different for Lisa? I figured I had done enough. I had lent her money once, and it had been a disaster for our relationship. I had supported her through her apprenticeship, both literally and emotionally. I was done. She should either get a job as a trainer, or work somewhere as an assistant, establish a track record, and work her way up, saving money along the way. She hadn't earned her stripes. I had been away from the office much too long. I caught a cab.

That evening I asked Lisa to meet me at a restaurant near my office. Lisa did not even bother to ask if Sam should come. She was used to the hours of a restaurateur. I had suggested we meet at nine.

As usual, when she walked in the door, a rush of wind and, I don't know, busyness seemed to accompany her. There was nothing quiet or calm about my wife. Wherever she went, she brought a bit of chaos rather than the serenity that actresses project when they play perfect wives. More Diane Keaton than Cate Blanchett, let's put it that way. Lisa was wearing a black suit, most likely Chanel, the jacket cut short and swinging as her hips moved. Four-inch high heels brought her up to my shoulder as we met to kiss perfunctorily. The hostess was all smiles as we were led to our table, but I promptly dismissed her and ordered our dinner, skipping cocktails. I wanted my decision laid out on the table.

I went through my thought process with Lisa, but she was not having any of it. "You cheap, controlling bastard," was where things started. She threw her fork down on the plate and left for the ladies' room. I'm sure she called someone from her cell to complain.

When she returned, I did not wait for her to get a word in. One look at her face told me that I would be in for a dirt-throwing barrage if I didn't intervene, so I said, "Time to grow up, Lisa."

"So that's your final answer?"

"Yes, you have to earn your stripes."

CHAPTER TWENTY-THREE

From that day until the one that marked the end of our relationship, things were never the same. Lisa rose early, often not saying good morning to either me or Sam, and she often did not return until the wee hours of the next morning. She went to the track at night in season, claiming she was researching horses with Simon.

On an unforgettable Thursday, I was putting away Lisa's less exotic underwear when I found a box from Harrods. I don't know what possessed me, but I opened it and took the silk shirt out of the box and held it up, freeing a pile of handwritten pages. I suppose another man would have kept his wife's privacy intact. In fact, I'm sure of it. But I am not someone else, I'm me, and with Lisa, I had to watch my back. And the truth is, I do have a need to know what is going on around me. I read enough to realize that Lisa had been consulting psychics about her future. Big deal.

But then I saw the card. It read: "Life without you is just not fun. I can't wait for when we'll finally be together all the time. Love, P." Amidst the rushing freight train of emotions coming towards me, I sensed some relief. Finally it all was coming to a head. What I had been feeling was reality. This card was confirmation and possibly the smoking gun I could use in time. I gathered up the card and all her psychic notes and put them in my car. I would keep these in my safe at the office. I drove over to pick up Samantha at school. A sense of relief came over me. I knew this roller-coaster ride was coming to an end. I would be entering a new chapter. I didn't even call Dave because talking about this would give it too much power. First I would act. Then I would feel.

In Drexler's office the next day, I heard what I already knew. There was little chance I was going to get custody of Sam. Joint custody was the best I could do, never mind that her mother was never home.

As far as the money went, I was looking at 40 percent of my income a month in child support and alimony.

"Take my advice. Speak to Lisa. Ask her what she wants. Don't argue. Write down what she asks for, and then we'll go from there."

I was at the numb part now. Soon I knew the feelings would come, and I wanted to be finished with the business part before I let the emotions start flowing.

A review of the numbers Drexler quoted only inflamed me more. I had been duped. Lisa had used me and used me well, but I would have to think about that later.

Drexler's office was near Giuliani's cleaned-up Times Square, so I decided to take a walk to nowhere. Truthfully, I disliked the new Times Square Disneyland with its shops for medieval devotees where formerly a man used to stand on a soapbox every day, screaming out that we'd all better find salvation or we'd be damned. I didn't miss the porn and the hookers, but they had simply relocated.

My thoughts went automatically to Sam. I would not duplicate the mistake I had made in my first marriage. I had fought for my son through the courts, believing there was some level of justice in the system. Having gone through this horrendous divorce and custody war before, I would negotiate my way through to the other side this time rather than go to the mat. I knew what the skirmishes had done to my son and our relationship. Thinking about that, I wondered what was best for Sam—would Lisa in fact be the better custodial parent? It mattered little, since Drexler was right—there was no chance I would get full custody. I wasn't going to look for what was fair this time. I would sidestep the judicial system and attempt to negotiate to keep the peace and keep Samantha from being damaged. I would hold my nose, ask Lisa for what she wanted, and give it to her. I found myself near the garage where I parked my car, my feet obviously way ahead of my brain. With Sam in school, I might find Lisa at Simon's farm or at home. Wherever she was, I would find her, and we would sort out our agreement. The time for venting would come later.

The West Side Highway was open this time of day, and soon I was on the Tappan Zee Bridge, a real looker of a structure. But today I was not admiring the view. My thoughts were on my daughter. How would I tell her the family was going to split up, that I would not be living with her full-time? How could I live without coming home to Samantha? A sob escaped from way deep in my heart and then another. Tears threatened to endanger the drive. On the other side of the bridge, I pulled over as soon as it was safe, and I allowed myself to let it out, the grief, sadness, rage, and the future longing for my daughter.

Shocked to find Lisa's car at home, I thought about the maxim that nothing happens by coincidence. As I entered the house, I knew I had the advantage at least in that Lisa had no idea what I knew. She would be totally surprised by me telling her that I wanted out. Drexler had advised me to push the memo button on my cell phone and tape the conversation. It was totally illegal, but it might serve to push her a little if she started to reverse herself later on.

Lisa was seated in the kitchen with a cup of tea and a racing form. When I walked in, she started, surprised by me being there. "You scared me. What are you doing home? Well, I'm glad you're here. I went to my lawyer today. I think we should split up. We've grown apart. I am not that twenty-three-year-old girl you first met. We want different things out of life. I've changed; I've grown."

Shocked, I sat totally still, waiting for the confusion and mixed emotions to stop swirling around. I decided to let her take the lead to see where the conversation went. "What do you have in mind, Lisa?"

Steady as a five-star general with a handgun, Lisa went to her purse, removed a piece of paper, and rattled off her conditions.

"I want my own house in Pleasure Valley. You can keep this one. I want enough money to buy everything I need to furnish it as nicely as this one. I want fifteen thousand dollars a month for the next two years so I can get my training business going.

"For Samantha, I want the same budget I have now. You'll pay for Samantha's school, extracurricular activities, and our health and dental insurance.

"I'll keep my car, my horses, and other assets, such as the jewelry you've given me."

I was speechless. Though it was less than the 40 percent of my income Drexler had quoted, at the end of the day, the cost would be the same. Who had come up with this detailed list for her? Certainly she had plenty of advisers, including "P," probably Nicole, and her lawyer. I felt like saying, "You'll get nothing, you cheating @#$%! I'll see you in court!"

But I did not say any of that. Instead, I asked about custody. I realized that I had not had the presence of mind to tape the conversation, so I wrote every word down in my day-timer.

"What about custody?"

"Joint custody is fine with me. I want Samantha to have a good relationship with you."

"What if your horse training business doesn't work? What then?"

"Then I'll have to get a job doing something else, I guess."

I waited a beat, as though considering, and then I said, "Fine, Lisa. This is fine with me."

She was caught off guard, probably thinking I'd give her an argument about leaving her. "Really? I never thought you would agree."

Not able to stop myself, I said, "You sound disappointed. I'm agreeing to this so long as we don't have to go to court. I want this to be an agreement handled by our attorneys. That's why I'm agreeing. If it goes to court, I'll take a different position."

"Oh, Bobby," she said, looking at me with those aqua blue eyes that had seduced me years ago. "I don't want another conflict. I want this over with as soon as possible. What happens now?"

"I'll get my lawyer to draft an agreement. Is Kara still representing you?"

"Yes."

"Let's not say anything to Sam yet. Please don't tell anyone in the community as it might get back to her. That would be a disaster if she heard it from anyone but us."

"Okay, Bobby. I'm so glad you're making this easy."

CHAPTER TWENTY-FOUR

I never mentioned the card or the psychic letters. I never asked her who "P" was. To be honest, it didn't matter to me. For all I knew, there may have been a series of alphabetical affairs.

It dawned on me, after discussing with Bill all the complexities of the legal procedures, that buying Lisa a home was not the best idea. He warned that family law always allows the parties to revisit the situation. I decided to call her father and meet with him concerning the financial matters of the separation. Though he hadn't answered my e-mail, I was certain that with his daughter's future economic well-being on the line, he would respond this time.

We met at a coffee shop near my office. We both ordered coffee. I was struck by how much older Ernie looked and bit my lip rather than ask him if he was ill. It was no longer my business, after all, though I liked the man.

After a few minutes of small talk about the economy and some jibes at the president, we got down to business.

"You know, Darlene and I are so sad about the breakup of your marriage. Sure you can't make it work?"

"We're sure." I refrained from telling him his daughter had been unfaithful. "But I'm worried about Lisa handling all the money she will get by herself. And of course, I'm worried about Samantha."

"You know we will always be there for Sam. As for the money, Lisa can come to me, and you know we're not a family that runs through money."

Well, that was a laugh. How to handle this? I figured the best way was straight-up. "My lawyer is afraid Lisa is going to come back for more later."

"Bobby, you don't have to worry about that. Lisa was not brought up to extort money or break agreements. I will make sure she respects your contract." Ernie stuck his hand over the table to shake mine. That was the best I could do. I was relieved that I could in good consciousness proceed with the agreement and move on.

###

Telling Samantha that her mother and I would be living in separate homes was the hardest thing I had to do. We told her together, and her reaction was as expected. She ran off to her room, crying. After five minutes, I went in to talk to her. I told her that she would always have her mother and father, just not at the same time.

###

Lisa did buy another house in the community. I negotiated the purchase price for her. Our agreement was for me to stay put, and Samantha could walk, ride her bike, and bring friends to both houses.

Lisa unilaterally enrolled Sam in after-school programs every day of the week. Between these activities and homework, the concept of Samantha floating between two homes was not the reality. When I called, the phone wasn't answered, and it went to message, even though I knew she was at home. In addition, for some strange reason, Samantha didn't want to come to the house. I bit my lip and was very patient. I thought this too shall pass and believed that things would work themselves out in time. I decided to focus on Bobby for a change. For the first time, I went to Europe—a three-week trip, the first time I'd ever been away that long. It was one big comparison restaurant tour. I must have gained fifteen pounds on that trip. I also went by myself, something I had never done before, and I thoroughly enjoyed it. I attempted to call Samantha at convenient times, but mysteriously, the phone never got answered.

As time went on, I received feedback from neighbors about what Lisa was communicating to them. I also heard from others what she was up to. The one horse that she wanted and I refused to "loan" her the money for was pale in comparison to Lisa's situation now. She now had five racehorses, and here was the kicker: she wasn't even training any of them. She had promoted herself to owner and hired trainers. All I could think of was how predictable her behavior was and how Ernie was far from controlling her finances as he had promised me.

###

Time passed, and the end of Lisa's two-year windfall of alimony was coming to an end. I was still frustrated with the lack of a set schedule with Sam, but I still bit my lip and didn't make a big deal about it. I had learned from my first marriage that if you make a big fuss over the amount of time you want, they'll just dig in and do the opposite.

Right on schedule, Lisa did the predictable thing and filed a motion for more alimony, child support, and to throw the signed agreement out as she claimed I made her sign it against her will, that she didn't understand what she was signing, and that I misrepresented my assets and income.

In Drexler's office, I met Max Geldorff. He was well-coiffed and had a serious but professional disposition. Max's background, I learned, was criminal law, and he had made the switch to family court. His background in the criminal arena had toughened his personality and made family law a walk in the park in comparison.

We all sat down in Max's professionally decorated office. Without any small talk, Drexler said, "I brought you here because we got served with papers from Lisa's lawyer's office. We're facing possible litigation. To bring us all up to speed, let me summarize what they're suggesting. Lisa's attorney is asking for spousal support and claiming you're a sophisticated businessman and that you 'duped her' when you didn't report all of your income. She was very stressed out, the cover letter explains, and didn't understand the conditions. Her lawyer goes on to say that you threatened to fight the divorce in court and told her she would end up with nothing if she did not accept your miserly offer.

"As a result, she's asking for the following: spousal support of thirty thousand a month; child support of thirty thousand a month, retroactive to date of separation; sole custody of Samantha; and she wishes to revisit the equalization payment."

To say I was shocked would be like saying that Vesuvius caused a really bad rock slide. I could not begin to give voice to my burning rage lest I scare away these two men who were trying to help me.

Bill asked if I wanted some water or maybe a shot.

Max interjected, "Bobby, this is a posturing position for the other side. They're claiming this to set the scenario for a bargaining platform. They want us to come back with something."

Bill added, "It's best to let Max take the lead here. Just knowing you've hired him will speak volumes to her lawyer."

Rather than trust myself to make a decision, I suggested that we regroup the next day.

CHAPTER TWENTY-FIVE

I started to walk. From Fifth Avenue and Forty-second Street, I did not look up until I was on Seventy-ninth and the Park. Since I had been beeped at by a number of cars because I did not see them turning, it was definitely good that I hadn't taken my car. Driving would not have been a good idea.

I found a shaded area and plopped down on a bench, where I replayed the events preceding the separation agreement. I remembered how I had held my nose and agreed to the crazy spousal support amount so that Lisa could get her career as a trainer going, which ended up to be an entire ruse. I had agreed to the child support she asked for. I had written Lisa a seven-figure check for her own home and furnishings, and all of this in record time. And since the separation I had found out she had put the house up for sale and sold it for a loss, claiming she needed the money to replace all she had lost on her racehorse business. In fact, she had given "P's" company four hundred thousand dollars from the proceeds of the house.

When I thought about bringing a motion to the court about this action, Bill had advised against it. I remembered all the court business of my first divorce and knew he was right. Divorce sucks you dry. But what other recourse did I have? I had been duped. Again. Lisa's fictions were predictable. She had been brought up with a lack of values and a lack of supervision over her finances, and I was paying the price.

Finally, logic kicked in. I had been able to take emotion out and look at the settlement as business before, and I would do it again. If insanity is doing the same thing over and expecting different results, then it would make no sense to give in again to her demands. I had given in to a thirty-six-page agreement, and she had spit back in my eye. I had given in to prevent us both from legal fees, and yet here I was, paying two lawyers, not just one.

No. Subject to Max and Bill's advice, I decided that I was not going to give her another penny.

A whole new energy started to build inside me. For the first time in a long time, I felt like my old self. With this new feeling, I started to prepare questions for the meeting with my lawyers.

But first I called Dave and asked him to meet with me later at a club he had been talking about. I knew my friend would help me see the light at the end of this hellhole.

CHAPTER TWENTY-SIX

The meeting was at Bill's office this time. Since it was an evening meeting, Bill didn't ask anybody what they wanted; he just walked over to his bar and poured drinks. The lawyers had alcohol. I stuck to Diet Pepsi.

"You look a lot better today," Drexler said, and I smiled.

"I feel good, and I'm ready to go."

"What are my chances of getting sole custody?"

Max answered, "That's a real uphill battle. Courts favor giving custody to the primary caregiver unless that person is a danger to the child. The fact that Lisa is a flake doesn't make it a reason to take away Samantha."

"What about the fact that she left the baby tied in her car seat all alone while she went riding?"

Drexler answered, "If that was documented and happened recently, yes, that would have been extremely relevant, but that was, what, six years ago?"

I processed this. Okay—so custody was off the list.

"We have a signed agreement. I gave her a lump sum and enough money for a small town to live on. That should have been plenty for her to get grounded."

Max stepped in to answer this one. "It's hard to analyze how a judge would see this. Under the law, a spouse is always allowed to petition the courts to review spousal and child support. The judge could go either way on this. The judge might interpret the spousal support either as a contract or as Lisa simply applying for money because she has greater need."

"But she squandered the money. She bought racehorses and didn't train other horses. She pissed it away. Who knows how? It would be insane to give her more."

"I think you have a strong argument, and there is precedent, but it's a toss-up how the judge will see it," Max said.

My good energy was dissipating as I moved to the last item on the list—child support. Max complimented Bill on doing a great job with the original negotiation. Then he said, "Here's the quandary, in a nutshell. Lisa's lawyer will say that, based on your stated income, you are paying less than the guideline amount even though you gave her a lump sum. Again, this is open to the judge's interpretation."

"But the money is exactly equal to what I gave her when we were together. Isn't that relevant?"

Again, Max answered, "Her attorney will argue that it's not. The judge will look at your income and see that you earn ten times what the judge earns. Usually, there's not a lot of sympathy for a person who makes that much money."

I could not hold back my anguish from these two men who were actually on my side and yet giving me such horrible news. "I gave her everything she asked for and more. She was cheating on me. When we decided to break up, I tried to avoid litigation. I did this so we wouldn't have to go through the courts, to keep us from being at each other's throats. I didn't want Samantha to see it get ugly. Look where it got me. By giving more child support, it's just going to give Lisa money for her horse addiction. Samantha won't see a penny of it."

I looked at each man individually and said, "What do you advise me to do?"

Bill went first. "I would much rather have an agreement in place than not have one. This is your position, that an agreement was done and that the courts should honor that agreement. The other side will try their best to punch holes in that argument, and you know what they'll say—that you bullied her, and so on. You can allow Max to negotiate with them for a more reasonable amount."

I took this in, attempting to take the facts beneath the steaming place inside my soul. I felt like hell had lit up inside me and devils were dancing there, triggering demons. "Max?"

"Bobby, you're not going to like my options. But you're a businessman, and I want to get to the bottom line. My opinion remains the same as the day I first met you. You can pay me, or you can pay your ex. Either way, it's going to cost you. I can't suggest who you pay; that has to be your decision. It's also possible, though, that you'll pay both of us."

I thought about Dave's comment last night—how important it was to keep a sense of humor, or go down in flames. He would appreciate this. And then I started to laugh. I don't know what the lawyers expected—tears maybe, or screaming—but I suddenly found the situation hilarious, blackly comedic, even slapstick. Max and Bill were looking at me like they were afraid they might have to call a doctor, or possibly security.

I pulled myself together.

"So—this is how it works!" I said. "Welcome to our Gold Digger Nation."

GOLD DIGGER NATION:
PART TWO

If you are located in the Western world—you live in a Gold Digger Nation. Chances are, what you will read and learn here will be news to you. If you *are* shocked by what you read here, then I've accomplished one of my objectives. My other objective is to actually do something about the current state of Gold Digger Nations, and shift the pendulum back to its rightful place. Whether you are a man or a woman, if you are contemplating marriage or have a friend who is, or perhaps a son or a daughter, please take the information in this book into account before you *or* they approach the altar.

The Sharia/Gold Digger Pendulum

The Sharia laws are those adhered to by some in the conservative Muslim world, not only in the Middle East but in other Muslim communities throughout the world. One example of Sharia is what happens when a woman is found guilty of adultery. She can be sentenced to death by stoning. Those taking part in the actual execution can include her biological family: her father, brothers, and also the husband she betrayed. Those of us who follow Judeo-Christian tradition may be quick to condemn Sharia Law as "barbaric." We shudder to hear of this practice and think to ourselves how much more fortunate we are to live in our forward-thinking Western world with our values, morals, and just legal system.

On the other end of the pendulum's swing is what I call "Gold Digger Law." To compare, if a woman commits adultery in our Western world, she will most probably receive custody of the children and will be awarded alimony, child support, and 50 percent of the value of her spouse's worth during the length of the marriage. The court will advise her to come back if she finds the amount insufficient. Welcome to our Gold Digger Nation!

Somehow, there is a disconnect between our ethics and the laws and procedures in Gold Digger Nations. Can you imagine how our judicial practices are perceived in countries where Sharia Law is the law of the land? They only have to point to our laws and practices to justify and reinforce their traditions. To the Muslim world, divorces in this and other democratic countries must seem like a scenario out of *Alice in Wonderland*. As ridiculous and unjust as we view their divorce laws, they see ours as equally absurd.

Clearly, the pendulum has swung too far. By exposing our Gold Digger Laws and practices, I hope to swing the pendulum back to the middle, where it belongs, and to where it properly reflects our Western morals and values. We should condemn Sharia Law, but we should equally condemn our Gold Digger Laws.

In our "enlightened" Western society, the legal system overlooks the actions of either spouse whether they steal, cheat, break agreements, not pull their share of responsibilities, or even abscond with the children. We call this "no-fault" divorce.

We revere our system of government, our legal system, and our never-ending efforts to level the playing field for all, regardless of race, religion, creed, or gender. This is the privilege of life in a democratic society. I like to think we all hold these convictions and that democracy is based on our ability to elect representatives to mirror our belief system. I would like to believe that our justice system will punish those who don't play by fair and just rules and those who exhibit improper conduct. We believe that honest and fair contractual agreements should be protected by our justice system and that we are protected from thieves, con artists, fraudulent acts, and abusers.

However, such beliefs in our Western world are nowhere to be found in Gold Digger no-fault divorce laws or practices. My fear is that we as a society know about this disconnect from our core values and morals, but we have turned a blind eye or, even worse, have bought into this politically motivated agenda and have accepted it. We may agree that the pendulum has swung too far, but we blame ourselves for this happening and therefore justify the inequity.

When laws and practices do not follow our code of morals and values, we are on a path to their complete erosion. When we have a system that can actually reward divorce, we have a Gold Digger Nation. What's the next thing we're going to reward? This concept is foreign to our beliefs and character as a society. There are no degrees of wrongdoing.

Either something is just or unjust. The fact that the ones being duped might be well off should not be a factor, even if those situations represent a minority of instances. Substitute millionaires with any other group and one can clearly see that we have a serious problem in our society. If we don't adhere to our Judeo-Christian morals and values, then our justice system is flawed.

Gold Digger Law is causing a ripple effect through our society, with serious implications. When you overhear a group of college-aged girls discussing what career paths they're going to choose, and one says, "This is too hard. I'm going to marry some 'dupe,' divorce him, and live a life of luxury without having to work," and they all laugh at this—the joke is on us as a society. The joke is on us because not only do we allow this, we welcome their conniving schemes without any questions asked. The vast majority of us have no idea what we're potentially getting into when we innocently walk down the aisle and enter the institution of marriage. Be afraid; be very afraid! Read on.

No-Fault Divorce

In the late sixties, seventies, and early eighties, most of the Western world adopted the concept of "no fault" in divorce proceedings. By doing away with the old system where the courts required grounds for divorce that included an attempt to determine who the guilty party was, the courts now simply said, "Who cares whose fault it is? There are two sides to every story, and does it really matter who's at fault? Let's just deal with the financial matters and custody." The family courts turned into courts of redistribution, foregoing justice.

No-fault divorce is a fallacy. What the courts are really saying is, "We know whose fault it is. Who else could it be other than the husband? After all, husbands are adulterers, deadbeats, abusers, bullies, sexual predators, sexist clods, and, thus, quintessential villains. Whereas wives are the natural caregivers, maternal, abused, living in a man's world, the weaker sex, cheated upon, and exploited in the workplace by not receiving equal pay for equal work, and, thus, quintessential victims.

So there we have it, folks, the poor little victim vs. the big bad villain. The courts concluded, "Why are we wasting our valuable time on fault? Let's get to the business at hand of transferring monies, assets, and custody."

Changing to "no fault" did away with the assessment of blame for the breach of the marriage contract. This accomplished two things. It made obtaining a divorce simple, as you no longer had to provide any reason for breaking your contract. In fact, you can now declare the marriage over unilaterally. Secondly, it did away with the uncomfortable and sometimes embarrassing aspects raised at trial to determine fault.

This action opened the floodgates and increased the number of divorces in the U.S. Marrying for money took on a whole new meaning. Not surprisingly, there is a strong correlation between who is likely to be awarded custody of the children (nine out of ten times contested custody goes to the mother), and who initiates divorce proceedings. Two out of every three petitions for divorce are initiated by women, according to Stephen Baskerville in his book, *Taken Into Custody*. In Canada, it's three out of every four petitions according to Statistics Canada.

There's an inherent bias in the no-fault system. It is well known in the divorce industry that the phrase "best interest of the child" is a code name for custody for mothers and all the trimmings that go with a custody award. With nine out of ten custody battles going to the mother, you can only imagine how much the tenth mother must have messed up not to get custody. It's not hard to see this bias.

The concept of the "mother" holds a long-standing role in our culture. To reject or not support a mother's position in custody, child support, alimony, and property distribution is uncomfortably close to rejecting one's own mother. In our society there seems to be a chivalrous duty by the courts to protect the quintessential victim from the quintessential villain. We're not supposed to have double standards in law, but we're talking Gold Digger Law here. Justice has been replaced with what is "politically correct."

No-fault divorce ended marriage as a legal contract. It turned marriage into a disposable product like razor blades, coffee cups, and shredded paper. In all forms of justice, we seek to identify and penalize a guilty party and protect and indemnify the non-guilty party. To not dispense justice is to promote injustice. Marriage is the only contract wherein the court sides with the one who wants to violate the contract (two out of every three petitioners are the recipients of custody, child support, and alimony) rather than protect the one who is abiding by the contract. Welcome to our Gold Digger Nation!

The Divorce Industry

Divorce is big business. How big? Try thirty billion dollars a year in the U.S. alone, according to Baskerville when adjusted for inflation. There are a lot of politically influential professionals with vested interests in protecting the status quo and the comfortable lifestyles that divorce proceedings reward them with. This group is primarily made up of lawyers, who reap the largest rewards, and psychologists, evaluators, judges, mediators, enforcement officers and agencies, forensic accountants, and court officials. Politicians have used divorce, specifically by beating up on so-called "deadbeat dads," to make political hay with women.

That's quite a formidable opponent we're up against if we want to swing the pendulum back into balance. When one raises the question of injustice in the present system, parties with a vested interest respond, "Well, there are cracks in the legal system, and a very few fall through the cracks."

Cracks? A black hole would be a more accurate description. After all, a million people are thrown down this hole every year in the U.S. alone, says Abraham in his book *From Courtship to Courtroom.*

In family law, there is a great divide between law and procedure. The law may be in English, but the procedures are in a language that only the lawyers and the rest of the divorce industry can understand. As anyone who has gone through the family court system will tell you, you are entering uncharted waters where your ability to swim, tread water, or attempt to paddle through white waters become non-factors. This makes representing yourself without a family law attorney—and their hefty price tag—extremely difficult, frustrating, and humiliating. I believe it is specifically designed this way to protect the self-interests of the court and the family law fraternity. Alec Baldwin's quote in his book *A Promise to Ourselves* brilliantly describes the court process as similar to a Vegas pit boss, whose job is to keep you at the table until you've dispensed with your funds. Family court is not a court of law, but rather a court of redistribution. It redistributes property, monies, and children. Silly you! You thought it was a court of justice.

How did it get this way? The most powerful influence on where we are today with this issue has been the feminist lobby, armed with some questionable research reports. The feminist movement is well organized, well funded, and influential. It has been extremely successful in influencing legislators, and the public, to a lesser extent, by portraying women as victims. Feminists have framed the institution of marriage as a patriarchal institution that suppresses women into subservient roles for the benefit of men. For two generations, a culturally triumphant feminism has validated the movement of married women away from homemaking and into the workplace, all the while characterizing traditional marriage as a patriarchal institution that represses women.

They are excellent at voicing their message: women are victims; men are villains. In her book *Who Stole Feminism,* Christina Hoff Sommers exposes how feminists have used bogus studies and flawed statistics to influence their agenda. They were able to influence lawmakers with some biased studies. My favorite study to illustrate their use of bogus statistics is a study showing how post-divorce women's income plunged 73 percent, while men's incomes increased 42 percent, as cited by Sommers in her book, *Who Stole Feminism.*

Think about that and the gullible legislators who bought this. Logic suggests that, if this were true, men would be lining up around the courthouses to get divorced to increase their incomes by 42 percent post divorce. Christina Hoff Sommers contends that this study was deeply flawed. It was a handpicked sample of a small group, held in one locale, and from women with major gripes about their awards, and it focused on the first year after divorce. Further investigation by Sommers revealed a blatant mathematical error, showing that the 73 percent decrease was really only 30 percent. To this day, politicians use these incorrect statistics to legitimize their support for the status quo.

The Gold Digger Nation transformation began in the seventies when the feminist movement and liberal left, armed with their flawed statistics and gender stereotypes, commenced lobbying for more child support, more alimony, and more of everything. Using the significant increase in poor unwed mothers as their rallying cry, they painted an ugly picture of men as "deadbeat dads." Politicians concerned about the large obligation of government welfare offices instantly allied with the feminist movement, which was becoming more influential with the female vote. Those who didn't go along with their agenda were labeled chauvinist pigs, cavemen, and anti-women. This was a powerful statement from a powerful organization.

Since the eighties, we've had a new scapegoat—deadbeat dads. Politicians found it advantageous to beat up on this small group and reap the benefits of the female vote and the feminist lobby's seal of approval.

Christina Hoff Sommers researched the realities of the so-called deadbeat dads, and she appropriately renamed them the "dead-broke dads." The vast majority of men behind in their support payments just couldn't afford to make the payments due to changes in circumstances. Only a few were those in a position to pay support but chose not to, according to Stephen Baskerville in his book, *Taken into Custody.*

When no one was looking and with very little attention, legislators overhauled the family law court into a court of entitlement that punished the stereotypical villains for the benefit of the stereotypical victims. To do this, feminists painted two vivid pictures. The first was the middle-aged, frumpy housewife and her 2.5 kids who were jilted and abandoned for a younger, sexier, and more vivacious home wrecker by her selfish and no-good husband. The picture was so vivid that you could envision the husband driving off into the sunset in his shiny red convertible with his new young love, leaving the woman and the 2.5 kids with nothing. The "victim" was also the one who put him through school, cooked, cleaned, and sacrificed her own career to give him a family, a house, and other subservient services.

The second picture the feminists painted was the woman with children, saddled with a life of poverty, and now a burden to the state as a welfare recipient. The father of the children had abandoned them, refused to recognize his obligations, and moved on to impregnate other women.

Legislators saw these two pictures perfectly and bought this hook, line, and sinker. Now with blinders on, and clearly with these two images radiating in their minds, they passed all kinds of family law "reforms" based on the feminist agenda, and they gave the family courts the power to execute their procedures.

The biggest changes were the introduction of "no-fault" divorce, and changing the role of alimony from a concept of a bridge to self-reliance, to one involving more complex issues and more advantageous rewards for women in some jurisdictions. Legislators bought the entitlement logic, and they adopted the concept of equal partnership in marriage, and thus the claim to 50 percent of net family income regardless of who created this value or how much it was.

Child support was changed from one of need to the concept of ability to pay. The legal profession put together guidelines so there would be uniformity in awards, making it much easier for them to work with and estimate based on the income of the payer. So now it wasn't based on a child's needs, but only on a percentage of the paying spouse's income. With blinders on and the feminists at the reins, this galloping horse and wagon express was ready to roll right over the patriarchal institution of marriage and the villains responsible for it.

Of course, the big winners were those who had "hooked" a good provider. Thanks to these new family law reforms, the family law courts were the new ATMs for the recipients.

With the new child support calculations, many recipients received an incredible windfall. With child support guidelines in hand, the focus was clearly on that cheap, cheating, money-hiding villain. The divorce industry ratcheted up their efforts to find and shake down this villain to give the entitled victim her maximum share based on the new guidelines. Women, who were the vast majority of the recipients, rejoiced over their new-found monies. Rather than awarding support based on a child's needs, they were free to spend these funds any way they wished with no control from the courts and no one to answer to. It amazes me that literally billions of tax payers' dollars are spent on hunting down, verifying entitlements, and greasing the money wheel of transfer of funds from primarily men to women. However, zero dollars are spent to ensure that child support dollars are actually spent on the children—the so-called intent of the transfer of funds in the first place—and not frittered away by the recipient. Deadbeat dads? No, entitled princess allowance enforced by the eight-hundred-pound gorilla under the disguise of child support!

The same became true with alimony. The feminists had created a jackpot for Gold Diggers so they could live in the same lifestyle standard as prior to the divorce, receive funds for that period of time required to enter the workforce (if that scenario was realistic), and last but not least, receive monies for "back pay" for missed opportunity while being married to the villain as a return on their human capital during their servitude, also known as marriage. In Canada, a family court judge can use any or all three of these scenarios to award Gold Digger entitlement. And they do! Oh, Canada…a Gold Digger's paradise.

Lawmakers created this entitlement frenzy off of the backs of poor people who never received the benefit of these large awards, because a percentage of income was used as a guideline. These poor souls, the poor and lower-middle-class recipients, made the horrible mistake of not marrying well. By marrying better providers, their well-heeled sisters hit the lottery off of their misfortune. With blinders firmly in place, no one looked at those higher up the income stream. And if they did, who cared? Who was going to feel any sympathy for a bunch of millionaires? Gold Diggers rejoiced and giggled all the way to the bank.

While legislators passed these laws, which were supposed to bring uniformity and fairness to support awards, there was no public debate, no front-page media announcement, no opposition. They were ushered through the system under the auspices of political correctness and modern progress. Lobbying groups with self-serving agendas, akin to the divorce industry, heralded the new reforms and took an active role in working out the details. As they say, "the devil is in the details," and this was the case here as well.

For the father who doesn't just agree to passively sit by—while he sees his kids taken away; the house with all the improvements he made, gone; half of the net worth during the time he was married dispensed; claims on his future income; and reciprocity for exploiting his ex during the tenure of the marriage—his option is to go to court. If he does this, his divorce will be labeled an "ugly divorce." He will be perceived as a maverick combatant and, chances are, he'll lose. For doing so, he will pay two lawyers, his and his ex's, because he lost. The legal bill(s) can be staggering, making the risk of litigation that much higher. Men are counseled to "shut up and pay." Welcome to our Gold Digger Nation.

Benefiting from Divorce

What if I told you that our system actually rewards divorce—would that alarm you? In Western society, our courts have made it so easy and attractive to break the marriage contract that in many instances you can actually benefit from divorce. Marrying for money is one thing (I'll call this minor league gold digging), but divorcing for even more money is clearly the definition of a Gold Digger Nation.

By creating this incentive, it is not a far stretch to see why our divorce rate has climbed drastically. We have emboldened applicants (two out of three are women, and there are some jurisdictions that it is as high as three out of every four) with the confidence to seek a better situation than remaining in the contract of marriage. In a study in England, 50 percent of defendants in the divorce petition did not see the demise of their marriage coming. Divorce rewards are such in our Western society that those who believe they will get custody and thus receive all the benefits of divorce are the vast majority who file for it. Of course, you need a pretty good plow horse of an ex to be able to give you those perks.

It's not just the divorce community that sees this. In Britain, wives too cash poor to divorce are offered bank loans to finance legal costs so they can get their lucrative awards. Yes, in our Gold Digger Nation, divorce is blue-chip bankable!

By framing divorce as women fleeing the oppression of the patriarchal institution of marriage, the feminists have been able to communicate this as another "victim" being awarded her proper compensation for the subservience of marriage. They have even been able to convince male society that the "villain" must have done something wrong—or else why would she want out of the marriage?

With all the encouragement and sympathy due a victim, the custodial parent gets the kids, monies, a future cash stream, and the freedom to spend it any way she wants. She also gets the protection and enforcement of the entire legal system, including the police. This allows her to pretty much call all the shots concerning the children and to reduce their relationship with her ex, the father of the children, to the status of perhaps an uncle rather than a parent.

Women can now easily escape the uncertainties, hard work, and compromises required in a life shared with a working husband, by divorcing and controlling the funds with no one to answer to—not her ex, and not even to the court. Who said you can't have your cake and eat it, too? What is really surprising is why there aren't more divorces considering the bounty of goodies that are being dished out at our local family court. Welcome to our Gold Digger Nation.

How Gold Digger Law Affects Marriage

Knowledge is power. If we knew what was potentially facing us, fewer of us would get married. The sad fact is, we don't know. If we took twenty people—ten potential recipients and ten of their dupes—put them in separate rooms, and asked each group what are the financial impacts in the event of a marriage breakdown, I'll wager that eight of the ten potential recipients would know exactly what they'd get from our family courts, to only two out of the ten dupes. Yes, knowledge is power.

Let me explain what's in store for you. Once you say "I do," you now have a 50 percent partnership going forward. In addition, in many states and areas in the Western world, when you buy your home or if your lifelong partner moves into yours, they're also 50 percent owners of the house, too. In theory, the institution of marriage has made you legally one entity, since you're going to be together until death do you part or until your supposed lifelong partner unilaterally files for divorce. Your only lifeline is an agreement called a prenuptial agreement, which must be agreed to under specific conditions. Only 1 percent of newlyweds have a prenup, but more on this later. You're also agreeing to compensate your lifelong partner for her services as your spouse as a missed opportunity cost to her. This is somehow legitimized for the missed income she could have made if she wasn't in your servitude as your spouse. You're also agreeing to keep her in a lifestyle that you've created during the marriage—the variable being for how long. You may also have to finance some form of training to get your partner into the workforce. If you have children, your partner will be entitled to an ongoing percentage of your future income, regardless of whether your children need those funds or not. At the same time, you will have no say in how she spends your money, nor will the court hold her responsible for her actions. Why? Because she's your lifelong partner. The fact that she filed for divorce and unilaterally chose to end the marriage is inconsequential and has no bearing on the redistribution of assets and your income. Make perfect sense now? I didn't think so.

Would you fly in a plane as a passenger knowing that in the event of a crash you would end up in horrible shape, but the pilot would walk away unscratched and maybe even better off? Well, she's the pilot, and you, my dupe friend, are the passenger. The pilot is in complete control.

When you say "I do," you're making a commitment. But not all commitments are equal. It's like ham and eggs, where you're the ham and she's the eggs. Yes, you're both making a contribution to the meal, but it's not quite the same, is it? Her commitment is minimal. For the dupe, it's all encompassing. If we were to put a percentage on it, it would be so lopsided as to be no comparison at all. Not really a fair scenario, but as your family lawyer will eventually say to you, "It's your fault—you married her."

But it's your wedding day, and you're in love—or in lust—and of course you're convinced that she loves you as well. Why else would she take such a gamble, such a chance, such a commitment if she wasn't madly in love with you? You know why. Because heads she wins, and tails you lose—in our Gold Digger Nation. If you knew what you were potentially facing, well then, your lawyer's words would be right. Chances are you didn't know what you were getting yourself into. You're so lucky to be reading this now and being informed. Knowledge is power. The opposite is also equally true.

Once you've been pronounced man and wife, she's in control. Control is defined as follows: you have everything to lose, and she has everything to gain. Your lifelong partner knows what she is entitled to, and now that she is secure with the marriage license, she will have no problem informing you about the specifics of her entitlement in the event she decides she doesn't want to be your lifelong partner after all—or until you say, "I can't take this anymore." She will remind you of the alternative every time you don't deliver on her wants and desires. When you marry, you get one boss, but when you divorce, you get two—your ex and the legal system. That's one big eight-hundred-pound gorilla!

Because of Gold Digger Law and its ramifications, your marriage is affected from the get go. The same lopsided scenario that takes place in our family courts is now taking place in your marriage. How does this happen? Their backup is the legal system outlining what she will receive in the event she wishes to ever trade her marriage "package" for what's behind the curtain. It's not much of a gamble when you already know what's behind the curtain, and you will be schooled about what's behind the curtain, too.

When your spouse knows family law entitlement, she may plan her marriage to maximize potential entitlement in a divorce scenario. Here's what she could do. She won't work so as to maximize her potential alimony awards. She will attempt to maximize her standard of living by demanding nannies, maids, extravagant holidays, and expensive automobiles. She will try to have as many children as possible, as they'll turn out to be future walking annuities for her. She will try to persuade you to buy the most expensive home possible so that she will get 50 percent of it, if you divorce. She will constantly demand that you spend as much money as possible on her, either by your efforts to please or through ultimatums. If you don't give her what she wants, she will decide whether it would be more advantageous to divorce you.

Divorce begins to sound so good that it's worth marrying solely to acquire the benefits of divorce. The reality is this: the divorce benefits can start as soon as you're married.

Because her entitlements through divorce are legal, she will be reassured by her girlfriends, her family, and daytime talk shows that it wouldn't be legal if it was wrong. After all, she is the victim, and you're the villain. Not too many people say to their employer, "I think my severance pay is too much," or refuse to cash their check from the government for Social Security. Clearly the problem is the package of "entitlement" with which family law tempts petitioners for divorce. Quite simply, it's ruining the institution of marriage.

Gold Digger Law does not just affect divorce, with its ridiculous bundle of "goodies" waiting in the wings; it is held over the poor dupe during the marriage. If you want to stay married, you'll give her everything she asks for. For a dupe, giving her everything she asks for just may be a better option than facing family court, having to face the shame of a failed marriage, and being estranged from his kids.

Many do exactly this, and not just millionaires. In a recent women's magazine survey, only 38 percent of married people say they're happy in their marriage. Considering half are already divorced, that translates to more like 19 percent of all marriages. I believe that number is high.

It won't take you long to shake your head and be cynical the next time someone describes your bedroom as the "master" bedroom. Yeah right, master, as in masculine! You've got to be kidding. Welcome to our Gold Digger Nation!

The Worst Gold Digger

By now, you must be thinking about how you can possibly protect yourself. You might be thinking you will avoid any possible contact with anyone resembling a Gold Digger. I've got news for you, my potential dupey friend—you can't run, and you can't hide from the worst Gold Digger in the world. There is only one way to avoid her.

The worst Gold Digger is our family courts, dishing out entitlements and redistributing your assets. The only way to avoid this eight-hundred-pound gorilla is abstinence—marriage abstinence, that is.

Some folks are opportunists, looking for any easy way to get through life without earning what they get. These folks are true parasites. These are the same types of people who look to rip off insurance companies, abuse government programs, and take advantage of any possible situation for their own benefit, not thinking about what such malice might mean to someone else. They rationalize with something like, "Oh, they've got tons of money, and if I don't get mine, someone else will." Here's the irony. Outside of marriage and family law, there are actually laws against this type of fraud. Not so in our Gold Digger Nation. In fact, even with proof of fraud, it makes absolutely no difference to the entitlement awards in some jurisdictions.

Once married and educated in what kind of entitlement the family courts are dishing out at your expense, potential recipients morph into Gold Diggers. Why, you ask? Just like climbing Mt. Everest—because it's there. It takes a very special person to have the high moral values to say to their lawyer, "I don't want what the courts are going to award me; I only want what is fair." None of their antics would be possible without the existence of the biggest Gold Digger, our family court. Your wife may or may not have been a Gold Digger entering the marriage, but one thing is for sure—she'll end up a Gold Digger once she exits our family courts.

There are lethal people out there who know the system and will attempt to con you into marrying them, or they will attempt to get pregnant, solely to acquire the benefits of divorce or paternity. These are despicable people. But this would not be at all possible without our Gold Digger Law. In a nutshell, this is the essence of living in a Gold Digger Nation. Everyone is cognizant of what's going on, knows it's morally wrong, illegal in any other context outside of family law, turns a blind eye to the facts, and dishes out entitlements from the real victim to the real villain.

Some might define a Gold Digger differently. They may define her/him as anyone who marries for money—someone like Anna Nicole Smith who married an eighty-year-old while in her late twenties. Prior to marrying the billionaire, Anna and her fiancé entered into a contract, a prenuptial agreement, which outlined what she would receive upon his demise if they were still married. Her share was a half-billion dollars. You might be surprised by my response, but I don't see anything wrong with this. This was a prearranged contract between two parties, both with independent legal advice, and signed out of their own free will. That's a bona fide contract. If that weren't the case, neither would have signed the contract. Marrying for a better lifestyle is fine. Divorcing for money is robbery! The attraction of a better lifestyle is similar to the attraction of a physically beautiful person. Where it gets very complicated and tricky is that you can't divorce for money, gold digging, unless you first marry for money.

Remove the power of redistribution from our courts, and we remove Gold Digging.

Gold Digger Economics 101

I'm addressing the following to all you Gold Digger wannabes out there. By doing so, we can focus on the tactics that our legal system accepts. The first thing you have to understand in Gold Digger Economics is that a large loophole exists in your favor. This is the key to all aspects going forward. The loophole clearly put is: "Who cares about a bunch of millionaires or very well-off guys?" Certainly not the judge who will hear your case. The lawyers? They're just concerned about what their cut is going to be in all of this. The legislators? They're the ones who stacked the cards in your hand. They have no sympathy. Nope, no one cares about a bunch of millionaires you've "duped." You might be thinking, *Surely tricking, being deceitful, or acting like a con artist will be detected by a court of law?* You would be mistaken. You have a full and clear pass on your actions regardless of how treacherous and evil they are. You have to keep that front and center as you go forward toward your financial freedom. Going into a family court is an exercise in financial redistribution. The only question to be determined is "How much?" All the parties understand this. There's one winner, and that's you. How much will your jackpot be?

Marrying rich may have its advantages. Divorcing rich, thanks to our Gold Digger Nation, is a total win, to say the least. The system has made it so simple and easy to abscond with a big bag of money that you'll be convinced it's not Gold Digging—it's entitlement. Kind of like non-guilt Gold Digging. You'll swear there should be a law against this, but instead you'll most probably be saying to yourself, "Why didn't I do this earlier?"

Your goal is to become SARAH. This stands for "single and rich and happy." Divorce gives you the single status again, but this time you're rich, and because of the economic awards, you'll also be happy.

There are three components to Gold Digger Economics: 1) property distribution, 2) spousal support or alimony, 3) child support, also known as the golden annuity.

Let's discuss each one in detail, so you'll know what you're entitled to.

Property Distribution

As soon as you say "I do," you're now a 50 percent partner with your dupe going forward. That's right—you're his partner. The legal system has given you this status as the feminist movement and others were able to further the concept of equal partnership for married partners, regardless of the actual distribution of work or contributions in the marriage. While you're out shopping and lunching with your girlfriends (or boyfriend), you're equal partners with your dupe, while he's making the money. Of course, that's not the image the feminist agenda displayed when the legislators pushed through these laws, but as we said before, "Who cares about a bunch of millionaires?" Some of your sisters don't have it this way, but that won't be your concern. Their drudgery made it all possible for you, but that's their problem.

The formula that you want to concern yourself with is how much more value is there since you walked down the aisle? Whatever that increase is, half is yours. That includes the value in the house, his business, investments , any assets he bought during the marriage, and money in the bank. Your lawyer and his/her team will put him through a living hell to verify all his assets—a shake-down that will make an IRS audit look like a G-rated movie. This is the real Gold Digging, and you don't have to lift a shovel.

That house you nagged him so long for, and got him to buy, is now the matrimonial home. Regardless of how much he put in, it's half yours, baby. All your hard work in tricking him into buying it and, of course, all the incredible furnishings and improvements are half yours, also. Your strategy here is to maximize your house. Try and get him to buy the most expensive home and to put as much equity in it as possible. In addition, your overall goal here is to make sure he's making as much as he can. Convince him of the benefits of working hard for now; take short vacations or, better yet, you take the vacation and leave him at the office where he can make more money for you. Just in case your cash cow gets sick or dies, make sure he's got lots of insurance.

Spousal Support
aka Alimony, aka Maintenance

Once again you have to thank your feminist sisters for this one. Spousal support, or alimony, historically was meant to be support funds for a woman as a bridge towards getting back into the workforce—similar in concept to severance pay for an employee. Now it's a lot more involved, and it's more intricate, too. You have to check your specific locale's laws, as they do differ.

Spousal support has taken on a whole new complex set of conditions. In Canada, for example, where the feminist movement has been met with the most enthusiasm, there are three components to spousal support.

A) The test to mirror the same standard of living you had during the marriage. This means if the funds are there, you should be living in the same level of comfort that you did while you were married.

B) The concept of marriage as a forgoing of opportunity cost while you were in his servitude. This one translated means recouping funds that you could have made if you weren't married and had been working.

C) The old standby of supporting you while you get back into the workplace.

Spousal support is a real scam. The law is so vague that it really gives the judge carte blanche to use any possible combination to pass money from him over to you. It could be one or all three. Coming down the pike is spousal support guidelines from the same folks who gave us child support guidelines. Why? For the same reason as child support guidelines. It's easier for everyone in the Gold Digging business to determine the outcome of their wealth transfer. It just gets better and better for the recipient in our Gold Digger Nation!

You can help your situation by doing the following: Stay married as long as possible. Never work during the marriage as this will count against you. Never try to increase your educational level during the marriage; wait until after. Attempt to live as lavish a lifestyle as possible, and lastly, when it's time to state your desire to get back into the workforce, pick a profession or calling that will be the longest and costliest as possible. Not to worry—

the court won't hold you to this, in any event, but you'll receive the most in spousal support this way.

Remember, don't get married again unless you've hooked a better dupe as your alimony will get cut off if you remarry. If he remarries, he's not so lucky. He's still on the hook to you. But here's the real beauty of living in a Gold Digger Nation. If he does remarry and his new wife works, you can argue that he now has access to more disposable income and, therefore, your alimony should increase. Wouldn't that be a hoot to get his new wife to support you?

You may ask, "What if his income changes?" You forget where you're living. This is not a Gold Digger Nation for nothing. The courts will not look favorably at his actions. They will see him as attempting to squirm away from his financial responsibilities. If his actions are voluntary, the courts may very well say to him, "That's fine, but you have to pay her the same regardless." If they do adjust his payments, it will not be without a stern verbal lashing from the court that he has responsibilities, and that responsibility is you. According to Baskerville, in only one of twenty cases does a judge actually reduce his payment due to circumstances. The ex-husband's ability to change careers, start a new business, or do anything that may impede his historical income will not be looked upon favorably. In fact, your entitlements may very well keep him from realizing his desire to start that business he's always planned on, retire early, or take it a little easier.

Your conduct during the marriage is irrelevant in determining your entitlement. Even if you committed adultery, stole, deserted, or were violent, this will not affect your entitlement to spousal support. Heads you win; tails he loses!

Courts will not ask you to account for how you spend your money. They are so preoccupied with figuring out where he's hiding assets and his ability to pay, they don't have time or concern for how you may be squandering it. If you need more, your lawyer can always make application for more to see if you can squeeze more out of your dupe. The law perceives this as righting the wrongs of society in general, the wrongful acts of a patriarchal society exploiting women in servitude to men. How they got that while you were eating bonbons on the couch waiting for your massage, I don't know. Those feminists and women's groups are good!

This is your ticket to SARAH, single and rich and happy. Divorce can be the road to the easy life—all at the expense of your dupe, who is now your financial slave, enforced by the family courts.

Child Support

This is also referred to as the golden annuity. To really enjoy the benefits of our Gold Digger Nation, you should try to have as many children as possible.

Child support is not based on need. It's not even based on historical expenses. Child support is based on his income as a percentage. This is why it is referred to as the golden annuity—because it's a percentage of his income. Economist Robert Wills calculates that child support levels vastly exceed the cost of raising a child. This makes child support payments into an income source for you. Wills further goes on to say that studies show that only one-third to one-fifth of awards are actually used for the children. The rest, my Gold Digger friend, is for you. Even though the divorce law clearly states that both parents have an obligation to support their children, you, girlfriend, get a pass in most jurisdictions.

Courts did what governments do best. They turned child support into a "tax," complete with withholding mechanisms just like other deductions. If he doesn't pay, the courts can do one of the following: garnish his wages, slap a lien on his property, intercept tax refunds, discontinue his driver's license, suspend his professional/business permits, put his face on a wanted poster, and lastly, throw him in jail. Now that's a Gold Digger Nation! By calling this wealth transfer child support, it amplifies nonpayment as an atrocious, villainous action on the part of the "payor," when in reality, only a small percentage actually goes towards the entitled children.

In addition to child support based on guidelines—and the guidelines are referred to as the minimums for judges to award—your dupe must also pay add-ons such as medical and dental, day care, extracurricular activities, and even private schools. The kicker here is that the courts do not monitor how these funds are spent by you at all. That's right, you get all this money, tax free, and you can spend it any way you like.

A good thing to train your kids to do is have them ask their father for things like sneakers, clothes, and toys they want so that you have more to spend on yourself. Anything that he spends on the kids cannot be offset or deducted from his child support payments to you.

You might be thinking, How can he wiggle his way out of this one? What if he remarries, loses his job, or wants to go back to school to get more training? Ah, my naïve friend, you forget you're living in a Gold Digger nation. The court will hold him responsible for his child support amounts pretty much all of the time regardless of what fate brings him. If it's voluntary in any way, he'll be ordered to pay the same amount. If it's involuntary, he'll be lectured to about putting his kids first, even though the money is really going to you and your new boyfriend. It's all based on his ability to earn and not what he actually earns. Of course, if he happens to earn more—you guessed it—he'll have to pony up and pay more. In fact, you can go back every year to make sure that you're getting the maximum by checking his income annually. This is not only an annuity for you—it's an annuity for your lawyer, also.

The cornerstone of child support is custody. As long as you're the primary caregiver, and the courts are there to pronounce you as one, you'll get child custody. This makes you the beneficiary of all these awards, and it makes him the payor. Even if in the future you're making more money or you've remarried, he's still on the hook. And it's not just until the child is eighteen. If your child is going to university and/or post-graduate, yep, he's still on the hook. If you were an intact family, this wouldn't be an automatic benefit. Welcome to our Gold Digger Nation.

As long as you're not a drug user or a raging alcoholic, you'll get custody under the auspices of being the primary child caregiver, even if you had a nanny since day one. By having custody you not only get the financial rewards, you also get the control and the power that goes with it. Custody is really about asserting control over the non-custodial parent. When you get the children, you get the emotional, legal, and financial leverage that comes with them. It will be up to you if he gets to see his precious children or not. It will be up to you if you decide to move away so he can't see them very often. In fact, you may even use this as a bargaining chip to get even more money from him. The reason for this is because courts really don't enforce visitation orders—not without having to spend a lot of money going to court, and not without a few warnings thrown in. After all, you're the primary caregiver. What are the courts going to do to the caregiver of the children? You're the victim, and he's the villain.

Prenuptial Agreements

Some dupes will say they will only get married if a prenuptial agreement is executed. Simply put, a prenup will only affect the equitable distribution aspect of the entitlements, and in some jurisdictions, alimony. It cannot affect child support, custody determination, and in most jurisdictions, spousal support/alimony. The court has the power to review the "fairness" of the prenuptial agreement and adjust entitlements as they see fit. Prenuptial agreements are challenged all the time.

Here's the reality of prenuptials. This is a contract that has to be signed with individual legal representation, with enough time prior to the wedding, and with full financial disclosure. Presently, only 1 percent of married couples have a prenup. Many of the 1 percent are very wealthy, though. This contract is a give and take between two parties. Your lawyer will be very accurate in predicting what you're giving up by signing a prenup. He/she will be able to negotiate a very good deal but something less than what the courts may award. The reality is that our gold digger laws predicate the prenuptial agreement as the yardstick. Stray too far from this yardstick and it may be looked upon by the courts as unfair. In the Lisa and Bobby Lakeland case, Lisa's lawyers challenged the separation agreement claiming duress, and questioning the accuracy of Bobby's financial disclosure.

Here's the kicker. What you may give up in equitable distribution by signing a prenup, you might make up in alimony and or child support. The court can and has neutralized any property advantage that was bargained for. Why? Simply put, judges do not like prenups. They see it as a way of circumventing their authority and a lack of respect to them and the court. They may also view it as an easy way for the villain to get out of a bad marriage and wiggle his way out of denying his lifelong partner her prize even though she initiated the divorce.

If he demands you sign a prenup, not to worry. Your lawyer will negotiate a good deal with his lawyer. If it's too lopsided, it runs the risk of being thrown out as unconscionable. By doing this, it takes a great deal of the benefit of a prenup away.

There you have it. Gold Digger Economics 101 in a nutshell is simply a case of how much you'll receive from the court of financial redistribution, aka family court. You can maximize your awards by playing the system as outlined above. Your Gold Digging strategy starts very early in your marriage, and you have to stick to your master plan to reap the big entitlements they're dishing out. As many women say after, "If I knew I was going to get all this, I would have exited a lot sooner."

To My Son and My Daughter

To my son and daughter, I love you very much, but you're not a prince or princess. I've raised each of you to be a productive person in this world and in your own way to make a contribution to mankind. You should not be a burden to anyone or take advantage of a situation or any institution. You've been raised to treat everyone the way you would want to be treated yourself. Don't be a dupe or a Gold Digger! This section is meant for my son and daughter, and everyone's sons and daughters, brothers and sisters, and mothers and fathers.

What You Are Risking by Saying "I Do"!

You can always change careers and get retrained for a new job, but your decision to marry, and to whom, will determine if you live a happy life or the alternative. Yes, there's a lot at risk, and it's a decision you should not take lightly. Many careers require an eight-year commitment, so take your time when deciding on a more important decision—whether to marry or not and if so, to whom.

Now that you've read the story of Bobby and Lisa, which represents the most common gold digger/dupe relationship, you have a very good idea of what could happen. You know the odds are pretty close to fifty-fifty that you'll end up divorced. Only 52 percent of marriages reach their fifteenth anniversary.

If you have children and you get divorced, you're facing the possibility of spending a generation in and out of courts, fending off extortion from your ex and her legal entourage. You'll be her milk cow, working and being controlled by her and the courts. As you have learned, there is no way to protect your role as a parent. No prenup will protect you from the divorce industry, the endless parade of demands, requirements, aggravation, and the financial catastrophe that you will face. There is no lifeline in this arena. It's like playing a game of volleyball, but on your side of the court you're on a patch of quicksand. The only way to guarantee you won't be divorced is if you give her everything she asks for and more. That's right, your marriage will depend on keeping her happy and on her knowing that her standard of living will drop by being divorced. For hers to decline means yours will be eradicated.

If you're the breadwinner and out earning money to support the family, you'll have your children taken away from you and won't have any input on the major decisions in their lives. This will, of course, affect your relationship with them—if you have one at all. You'll adjust to not taking for granted seeing them until it actually happens.

Why is marriage risky? Because it's out of your control. In our Gold Digger Nation, one party can have the other summoned to court, without presenting any legal wrongdoing, and request that he be stripped of all rights over his children and ejected from the family—and a judge may do so without even asking any questions. Because of this, many men remain in unhappy marriages just so they can have a relationship with their kids. That's what you're risking!

Why Are *You* Getting Married?

This is a question I ask you, and it's the question you should ask yourself. More and more people, both men and women, are electing to forego the marriage "trap." Many see marriage as an irrelevant institution that was based on historical economic and social reasons that are not factors today. Regardless, there are still numerous reasons why people do get married. The reasons for marriage have been engrained in our Judeo-Christian ethics, morals, and traditions. Our Gold Digger Laws serve as a disconnect to this. This is where the problem lies. How can we on one hand define marriage as a lifelong partnership with all its trials and tribulations, its sacrifices and responsibilities, while our justice system has turned this into a gold-digging entitlement extravaganza for those unilaterally wishing to jump ship under the auspices of no-fault divorce? Can anyone really blame a cynical guest at a present-day wedding ceremony, knowing what it means to be married in a Gold Digger Nation?

In today's Western world, there's only one reason that you should ever consider getting married, and that's if you want children. All other reasons are weak ones. They're based on fears or personal weaknesses that one should face up to rather than attempt to smother by looking to someone else to fulfill you. Even though your reason for getting married is to have a family, there is no guarantee that you're going to have one in the future.

Some of the other compelling reasons are as follows:

Safety and security. Now you know better, as we're living in a Gold Digger Nation with marriages that are unilaterally disposable. So forget safety and security. If you're getting married to have a caregiver when you're older, you might want to rethink that concept. Security and entitlement is one-sided with no quid pro quo. This is why typically weddings are great days for brides and a very nervous one for grooms. If more grooms really understood the consequences, I believe they would be more than just nervous. They wouldn't show up! It is not a fear of commitment. It is a fear of our Gold Digger Nation.

For scintillating or steady sex. You'll be amazed how quickly this will likely diminish or outright disappear. Regardless of how frequent or wonderful it is now, as the joke states, wedding cake is the best birth control method there is. Due to the intricacies of the relationship, the new responsibilities, and change in lifestyle, it's just not what it was. On Dr. Phil's Web site he states, "Sexless marriages are an undeniable epidemic."

For an entertaining companion. People change and so do their interests. What was once a common thread may not be there in a short period of time.

For admiration or a cheerleader. I hate to burst your bubble, but the odds of that being there on a continuous basis is slim to none. If you need a cheerleader or admirer, you have your mom and your dad…that's about it for who you can count on.

The only positive reason to get married is to procreate and have a family. I have to say that having kids is not for everyone. Children are not all they're cracked up to be. I know it's not politically correct to say this, as one can be labeled a selfish monster, but it's an incredible, life-altering event that will last more than a quarter of a century. Not everyone is cut out to be a parent. You might not be so lucky as to have two wonderful children, like I did. You won't really know until it happens. But what I can do, and all parents should do, for their own children is to not pressure them into producing grandchildren for your own selfish needs and wants. I believe that there would be a lot fewer marriages and, therefore, a lot fewer divorces if we were not subject to any of the following: pressure from girlfriend/boyfriend, parents/society, and also non-planned malicious or accidental pregnancy.

Don't Get Married Unless…

Here's the real marriage vows test! Gentlemen, can you say "I do" to the following?

Do you, _____take_____to be your lawful wedded wife for all the benefits of marriage and none of the sacrifices, because she can unilaterally end the marriage at any time and for no reason, as she might be bored, unfulfilled, or might find it more economically advantageous, or may have found a better situation out there, or believe there is one out there, and that she can take your kids, half of everything you've acquired during your time together, even though it was you who earned it, your house, and while she may be with her new lover in a new city so you can't see your kids, you'll be supporting her with alimony and child support that may take up all your resources, which she can spend any way she wants, and if you don't pay you can go to jail, and she can also come back every year to try and squeeze more out of you?

If you can say, "I do," to that, then you're a very brave person. Realize that you're potentially hanging there by a string, and she's holding the scissors.

Of course, the actual wedding vows do not say what the reality of the justice system is. I would think that if more wedding vows were put into the real legal context, there would be fewer marriages.

But If You Still Want to Get Married…

If you can say "I do" to the Gold Digger Nation wedding vows, for whatever reason, then please follow these rules.

Pick a person with all the traits and qualities you would want in a person you'll be divorced to. This also may match the same qualities that will give you the best chance at succeeding in your marriage. Statistics show that the old-fashioned, traditional roles in marriage (yes, chauvinistic) give you the best odds of marriage success. The most risky are the modern-style marriages with both spouses having similar roles. Moreover, I believe, the following demographics and psychographics increase your chances of not appearing in divorce court. The following are results of research executed by the Australian National University.

a) Religious people who have this as a cornerstone of their daily life, who take their vows as a religious covenant, read the Bible, Talmud, or Koran, and reject modern society's values;

b) People who live a simple lifestyle, who live within or below their means and save money with a focus on quality of life rather than accumulation of material items;

c) People from certain geographical areas who hold customs and traditions of high values;

d) People whose parents care more about what's in your heart and your character than how you will be able to spoil their princess and perhaps themselves;

e) People who are not self-centered. This is a telling feature. Look for someone that is humble and grounded

f) If a husband is nine or more years older than the wife, it is twice as likely to end up divorced.

Husbands marrying under the age of 25 also have a very high divorce rate.

g) Children from a previous marriage also affect divorce. Almost twice the percentage.

h) If his or her parents were divorced, this has proven to be a factor in the outcome of their children's marriages.

I) Partners who are on their second or third marriage are ninety percent more likely to separate than spouses who are both in their first marriage.

Give the following test to your friend whom you suspect is headed down a path towards divorce court or unhappiness.

1. Is her belief system anti-male? She will see herself as a victim and eventually will see you as the villain.

2. Does she laugh at comics trashing men?

3. Does she have a negative attitude towards traditional women's responsibilities?

4. Does she look down at these traditionally female tasks?

5. Does she use sex as a weapon by withholding it? (This shows her as manipulative, as she views sex as a reward a woman gives a man. Chances are your friend will have a sexless marriage.)

6. Is she a financially responsible person? A key question is what kind of a wedding is she fantasizing about? Is she demanding and out of touch with the economic realities? A good omen is if she's more concerned with putting

funds towards the down payment of a house than spending it on a lavish wedding.

7. Is she controlling?
8. Does she try to change you?
9. Does she lay guilt on you and play mind games?
10. Does she have to prove that she's right? Does she have to prove anything? If she does, she's got some mommy-and-daddy issues that she'll transfer over to you to play out.

Any negatives in this test are not good. The more negatives, the faster you'll find your friend divorced, or just plain miserable.

Get a Prenup

Get a prenup. No ands, ifs, or buts…get a prenuptial agreement. The process of going through a prenup will speak volumes and be enlightening, to say the least. The prenup is not only a mandatory lifeline you may need in the future, it's also serves as an important test.

There are some areas that are not valid in law in a prenuptial agreement. My advice is to put everything in, regardless if it's legal or not—custody, child support, alimony, and of course the one area that is binding, property division. Why put it in if it's not recognized by a court?

Remember, your goal is to marry someone you would like to be divorced with. If that works, all other aspects should work out fine as well.

You're attempting to achieve two things:

1) Going through the exercise of a prenuptial is a test. You want to see her reaction to this agreement while the two of you are at the pinnacle of your relationship. Who she consults for advice is very insightful. If you find her to be vindictive, money hungry, or if she says, "Well that's what the law says I'm entitled to," and refuses to sign, you've just made the best investment of time and money in your life. That's your cue to run for the nearest exit and thank me for giving you this valuable advice.

2) You can use the prenuptial agreement to lay out and define your roles and responsibilities in the marriage, and if you divorce, what your continued roles will be. If she's planning on working, throw in how money will work between the two of you. Determine the protocol and rules on spending, and so forth. If and when children arrive, who does what, who works, who doesn't, and in the event of divorce, how time will be spent between the kids and the two parents.

If nothing else, you'll clear the air and have something in writing that you can refer back to when you're not so high on love. If you're planning on having kids, have your lawyer put in this clause: "It is our intention to raise our children as a partnership with the strong belief that children need both their mother and father making decisions for them. With all due respect to the court, no one loves our children more than we do, and therefore we do not relinquish our responsibility and our rights to give to the court the power to make decisions on our behalf."

Marry someone who is effortless and allows you to be you. Whom you marry is a more important decision than what you'll do for a career. Some career training can take up to eight years, so take your time and choose wisely. We change careers in our lifetime, but changing partners can be a lifetime of aggravation and pain. Your only reason to get married is to have children and create a family. Your spouse should be chosen on the attributes of being a good mother/father. There is a strong correlation between this attribute and being a good person. If you look specifically for this quality, you will minimize your risk of a painful and high-conflict divorce.

Here's the irony in all of this. The best possible chance of success in a marriage is also the most expensive divorce. This is due to the economic factors of having a "traditional" marriage. The least expensive divorce scenario is also the least likely marriage to survive.

We Have to Move the Pendulum

So, what's a poor dupe to do? The choices are to abstain and not get married, or hold your breath, jump in, and hope for the best. There are options to not getting married, and many men and women are choosing this route. My belief is that, until the laws are changed, you're taking an incredible risk with dire consequences if you marry today in our Gold Digger Nation.

To save marriage as an institution, we're going to have to change the legal system—not only the laws, but the procedures in the family court system. I'm not referring to a few tweaks here and there. Rather, I believe we need to have a full discussion on this subject, and it has to involve all parties concerned and not just the divorce industry players and the special-interest lobbying groups. If we don't make any changes to the status quo, we risk losing marriage altogether.

Government intervention in the affairs of private citizens who have broken no societal laws have gone too far. Legislation and procedures have sold out to the so-called political correctness of the feminist lobby and the divorce industry. No-fault divorce has proven to be a fallacy and is really just unilateral divorce.

There will always be a role for some intervention by the legal system in family situations. But what's with the existing "heavy hand"? The government should limit itself to cogent legal proceedings like enforcing contracts in the civil courts, dealing with violence under the criminal code, and focusing on abandonment of responsibility issues. What we have now is truly Orwellian. This has to stop.

As potential dupes learn about the incredible entitlements dished out by our family courts, I believe they will do the logical thing and abstain from marriage. In a free market system, we see how obtrusive laws have affected where people do business, and so forth. If the legislature views divorce entitlements as a "sin tax" and, thus, thinks dupes don't have a choice in the matter, I will add that it's a lot easier to say no to marriage than for a nicotine addict to give up cigarettes or for an alcoholic to give up drinking.

Under the auspices of chivalry, the legislature believes they are protecting women and children with ridiculous entitlements. They are doing so at the cost of the family as we know it. If the family is to survive as an institution, the major thrust of existing legislation must be altered. Many married dupes, faced with the realities of a gender-biased family law system (which nine out of ten times strip them of their parental roles with their children and awards absurd entitlements to their spouse), simply elect to stay in an unhappy marriage. They do this out of strength rather than weakness, as they will endure the unpleasantness of a failed relationship rather than be relegated to the status of non-parent with their children. This should not come as a surprise. Men have always, for the most part, made sacrifices for their children and for their country, too, for that matter.

In a study completed by Wallerstein/Blakeslee, only one in ten children experience relief when parents divorce. These were predominantly violence related, and with older children. Clearly, divorce is for the benefit of only one party, and that's the custodial parent, not the children, and certainly not the dupe. This is really who the feminist lobby is speaking for when the phrase "in the best interest of the children" is uttered. "In the best interest of the children" is code for custody for the mother…period! If we were honest, that phrase would be "in the best interest of the mother."

Returning the pendulum back to the middle may very well be the tipping point for us as a society. We have lost our way from what has made us successful in the first place. We have become a society of entitlement, and nothing says entitlement better than our Gold

Digger Laws. Our society is in constant need of instant gratification, which unfortunately means, "I don't want to work for it; I want the benefits now." Our no-money-down, have-it-now marketing schemes, our disposable marriages, and our Gold Digger Laws represent our unwillingness to work for something. The housing market crash and the huge credit card debt are part of the same bundle of problems. We don't want to work for it; we want it now, and we're entitled. I'll lay the blame for the housing market and the credit card debt on the marketplace, which just attempted to market what consumers wanted.

When it comes to the Gold Digger Laws, I'm blaming the legislature for allowing this to exist. By having the existing laws and corresponding entitlements available, what we're saying to people is this: "You don't have to try and make it on your own when you can latch onto a good 'plow horse,' divorce the dupe, and get all the benefits of easy street." Who does the divorce industry blame? They'll blame the dupe with the catch-all phrase, "Well, it's your fault—you married her." They'll do this rather than look at what it truly is—a flawed set of laws and procedures that are unjust.

Changing the pendulum to its rightful position will be the first step back to family values, our Judeo-Christian work ethics and morals, and to individual responsibility rather than looking to be bailed out by someone else. Yes, changing our Gold Digger Nation may very well be the tipping point in getting us back to prosperity financially, and also morally. If our rallying cry will be "yes we can," then I suggest we can only do it by changing our entitlement society back to one of work ethic, rewarding for hard work and ingenuity, and demolishing our Gold Digger Laws and all other "perks" that reward the parasites in our society.

Here are my suggestions for setting the pendulum back to where it should be. I hope that the following will serve as a starting point to get the dialogue going between legislature, organizations, and with you and yours at the kitchen table.

Custody: It's All About the $$$$

Change the custody bias, and all the rest will follow. Custody is the kingpin. The divorce industry—which includes lawyers, government agencies, psychologists, social workers, and mediators—has created a complex system to ensure that custody goes to the mother. They do this because to play along, you have to go along, and the divorce industry has set the agenda for them. The law states that both parents have an equal right to custody, so it's not a matter of changing the law, but rather to dismantle the divorce industry and their inbred biases, faulty research, and self-serving actions.

I don't want to go into great detail on the issues of custody, as so many experts in this particular area have already covered this in tremendous detail. The reason I bring it up at all is to show the link between custody and its associated award of child support. You can't get child support without custody. Let's follow the money!

Custody means control, and custody means child support. In the Britney Spears and Kevin Federline divorce, custody translated into one hundred thousand dollars a month to the recipient. Do you think it really mattered to either party which nanny was looking after the kids? Custody represented a windfall in child support. Follow the money!

The federal standard, not to be varied by state law, should be joint custody—also known as shared parenting. If there's credible proof of abuse and or violence, that should be dealt with like all other criminal matters. If one parent decides to leave the jurisdiction, that action should trigger a change for the parent moving and not the other way around. Put a stop to the acceptability of the practice that once a parent gets custody, they can move the kids away and thus severely impact the relationship with the other parent. With custody goes power—power over the other parent at the expense of the children, I might add. It happens on a frequent basis with nothing more than a civil reprimand from the family court. Oh, and it will cost you thousands of dollars in legal fees for the privilege of witnessing this, if you're so inclined.

When joint custody or shared parenting is the default template, as it is in some jurisdictions, divorce rates plummet, according to Stephen Baskerville. Professor Edward Kruk, a University of British Columbia sociology professor, stated in a research paper that a minimum of 40 percent of a child's time should be spent with a parent to maintain a beneficial attachment. Most non-custodial parents get maybe four days a month with their child, and some holidays, which might add up to about 20 percent of total time together with their children. The current psychological position is, "We can't divide the child in two like King Solomon suggested; therefore, the primary caregiver, which is code for the mother, should get sole custody." If one argues for joint decisions on issues for the children, the mother has only to say, "We don't communicate well," and that gives the court ample reason to award sole custody to the mother. Seems to me that the courts should be representing the position of the parent who wishes to get along rather than the alternative, but such is not the case in our court system.

The reality is that sole custody pushes fathers out of their children's lives, and that should not be the objective of our society. There are all kinds of data that support the scenario of what happens to children without a father's involvement, and it's not good. The objective should be the exact opposite. It should be the role of our courts to ensure that both parents continue to have a parental relationship with their child, and they should enforce that, rather than the other way around. Society should demand this, and courts should protect this irreplaceable and crucial bond. Instead of ripping children from their fathers, the obvious requirement should be, "I need some very compelling and indisputable reasons why these children should not have a strong and meaningful relationship with their father."

If you follow the money, you'll see why women want sole custody. If you are aware of the power they have over their exes, you'll understand why custody is the prize in our Gold Digger Nation.

The Child Support Annuity!

Most of the Western world has adopted a system of guidelines for awarding child support to mothers. It is not based on a child's needs at all. Rather, it's simply a percentage of the father's income. The more you earn, the more you pay. Of course, these guidelines are only the minimum that can be awarded. If the mother can prove that for whatever reason these sums are insufficient, the court may order more. The divorce industry adopted these guidelines under the auspices of equality in award amounts regardless of which judge was presiding over the case. Sounds good, doesn't it? Robert Wills stated in his findings that only one-third to one-fifth of the child support awards is actually required for the child's needs. The rest is simply alimony in disguise. In very large awards, that number could be one-twentieth!

On the lower end of the income scale, guidelines do make sense as a percentage of a parent's income. When the divorce industry came up with their formula, it was based on low-income earners and their ability to pay without pushing them into homelessness. In New York State, for example, the first child represents 17 percent of a father's income. If there are more children, the percentages increase. All this sounds just, until you climb up the income stream. I should mention that some states do have a ceiling rather than a straight percentage of a father's income. This at least limits the charade of calling it child support.

Now with guidelines in place, the rules of engagement have been set. The mission is for the mother—who nine times out of ten is the one who receives custody—to engage a team of forensic accountants, evaluators, auditors, and lawyers in an attempt to attack the dupe with intense probing, dissection, interrogation, and hacking to squeeze out and or inflate the highest possible income number that the courts may use for guideline application. Because this is an award for the mother, it explains why so much time, effort, energy, and money is involved in this exercise. Follow the money, and you'll understand the workings and motivations of the divorce industry and the recipient. This, of course, is all under the guise of "the best interests of the child."

Get this! Once the funds are awarded to the mother, the courts wash their hands of their responsibility. She is responsible to no one for how she uses the funds. The children can go without while she uses it for her new boyfriend, and the courts will turn a blind eye. If you bring a motion to the court, the judge may very well look to you to pay even more since you're complaining that the children have needs.

By calling it child support, it has all the trappings of "the best interests of the child," and who's going to argue with that? The reality is that we know how much it costs to raise a child. All kinds of government studies report on this specific issue constantly. According to the U.S. Department of Agriculture, for families earning north of seventy-five thousand a year, the cost of raising a child is nine thousand dollars a year after the housing allowance. Included in that sum is health care, transportation, food, clothes, school (not private school), and miscellaneous expenses. For the lowest quartile, the government has established the figure of 388 dollars per month for a child. This is how much the government awards a child of a welfare recipient. If a child needed more, don't you think the government would give more?

Now that we know how much it costs to raise a child, can we please stop trying to call any amount over this anything other than alimony?

The feminist lobby and legislators have joined together to attempt to paint the picture of fathers as "deadbeat dads." Only 4 percent of fathers making over forty thousand a year are behind on their child support payments according to Baskerville in his book, Taken Into Custody. Considering that the unemployment rate is higher than that, I think this statistic shows fathers as responsible individuals, even when duped into paying more than is required for their children. I believe it is fair to say that most fathers have no problem living up to their responsibilities of looking after their children. Guidelines have turned this altruistic responsibility into a child tax to benefit their exes. When we pay taxes to the government, we at least get an accounting of where our tax dollars are going, even if we don't agree with the allocation. That's not the case in our Gold Digger Nation.

Therefore, child support payments from one parent to the other should not be based on a percentage of after-tax income, but on a child's needs. Here are my comments on how to make this just.

Records should be kept of expenses during the marriage of what was spent on the children to use as a backup to the government's own statistics. If child support was simply that, and not a built-in alimony annuity, we would be taking away a huge incentive for the mother to commence with divorce proceedings. This fits perfectly with the joint-custody or shared-parenting model that we discussed earlier. The end result would be less incentive to divorce and, therefore, fewer broken homes for children.

Alimony, Spousal Support, Maintenance

If divorce is truly "no fault," then alimony in its present form has to be changed. When a marriage is over, the benefits of marriage should terminate. Modern alimony awards can literally award all the same benefits of marriage to a cheating, stealing spouse under the no-fault clause. Is this absurd, or what? This is so contrary to our morals and values, it's worth repeating again. When a marriage is finished, the benefits of marriage should be finished as well. If not, then it makes a mockery of the institution. The bridegroom is not so much afraid of commitment as he's afraid of a lifetime of financial slavery, which is enforced by the eight-hundred-pound gorilla of a legal system.

No fault means, "Look, we tried, and for whatever reason it didn't work. It's no one's fault more than the other, so let's each go our own way and all for the best. We'll split the assets we've accumulated, even though it was me who earned them, but that's okay. Have a wonderful life."

This was our understanding of what no-fault divorce was all about. The court was not going to lay blame on who broke the wedding vows any longer and was going to focus on the rest of the matters. With a marriage contract or prenup, this is acceptable and workable. But what doesn't correspond to no fault is the three levels of alimony awards. We have already discussed how the feminist agenda has lobbied in this arena and made this a clear "heads she wins; tails you lose" scenario for the dupe. Nothing irks a dupe more than the concept of alimony, and here's why.

When a man and a woman became a family, in the vast majority of marriages, she benefited from the increased lifestyle level that resulted from the marriage. She wouldn't have lived in the kind of house, in the kind of neighborhood, driven the type of car she kicked around in, and she wouldn't have had the wardrobe she has now, gone on the type of vacations, and seen the world in the same way. She wouldn't have been able to live a non-work lifestyle the way she did, avoiding rush-hour traffic, the pressures of having to produce, being responsible to various people, experiencing the anxiety of meeting projections, deadlines, payrolls, and paying all the bills. She wouldn't have been able to go to the gym every day, spas and hair salons and nail boutiques, and have lunch with her girlfriends and attend social gatherings. Now, our Gold Digger Nation says the dupe should compensate her for the lost revenue she could have earned if she had worked. He should compensate her under the auspices of subordination in a patriarchal society. Excuse me? Are you kidding me? How about you write me a check and reimburse me for all the money I spent on you? Nothing makes a Gold Digger giggle more than the concept of alimony when she's discussing this with her girlfriends. It's the ultimate "gotcha!"

Alimony, in isolation from all other awards and issues, should at the most be only for a transition period for the purpose of being trained to enter or return to the workforce. The cost of training or retraining should be looked at in a universal award context and not as individual "entitlements" like a shopping list. Alimony in its present form does not put any restrictions on how the funds can be spent. She can use her alimony for getting a boob job or going to Vegas with her new lover.

To award alimony, other than the absolute minimum, is to make a farce of the concept of the term "no-fault" divorce. Alimony is used as a penalty against a predetermined guilty villain and to reward a perceived innocent victim. How is this possible under the concept of no fault? If that's no fault, then bring back the draconian divorce trials to determine fault. That system at least had some semblance of justice. What alimony translates into in modern-day family court under the "no-fault" banner is that we've determined who's at fault, and it's your fault, dupe.

The bottom line is that we should change the award of alimony from its current practices played out in our family courts to one of true no-fault divorce, and you'll see the divorce rate drop, and we'll keep children in intact families. All you have to do is follow the money!

Make Prenuptial Agreements Mandatory

The cornerstone to my views on reforming current methods and protocols is to completely overhaul the prenuptial contract. Only 1 percent of all marriages presently have contracts. I'm suggesting that 100 percent have contracts. A prenuptial agreement is presently solely for the benefit of the dupe as the intent is to protect his assets going forward in the marriage.

We have it all backwards. The reason it's backwards is because of the existing position in divorce law. Algebra is the *only* place where two negatives equal a positive! Instead of having the dupe state what he wishes to protect, a mandatory prenuptial should state what the non-breadwinner demands in the prenuptial. This would only work if we change the current procedures and practices.

A good comparison would be an employment contract. In some jurisdictions, employment law, in the event of dismissal, firing, quitting, layoffs, and so forth (does this sound like no fault?), regardless of the reason, the employee shall receive one week of pay for every year served. This is known as severance. Other governments may have subtle variations to this. An individual employment contract can provide greater benefits. Setting the bar at a low level is done with the intent that the severance amount is a resource for an individual to get to the next step. However, some employees have negotiated employment contracts with a much more generous package than anything the government sets. We have heard more about these employment contracts in the form of "golden parachutes" for Wall Street CEOs and other executives. There are instances where certain individuals receive astronomical amounts of money as a severance package even though their results were less than stellar—they even may have overseen the demise of the company.

Imagine, if you will, that there was no contract in place and the courts dictated to these companies that, regardless of these CEOs' results and or their duration—never mind that they put the company into bankruptcy and may have caused millions of stockholders to lose their savings and retirements, caused thousands to be out of work and millions of potential losses for suppliers—that they had to pay these individuals some ridiculous amount of money on top of the hefty sums they earned in salary. If this were the scenario, you would have our existing Gold Digger Law dished out by family courts now spilling into civil law. There would be riots in the streets!

The difference between this scenario and what we have now, what is now played out in our family courts, is that one was a contract between two parties with no government interference except to guarantee the validity of the contract, and the other is the government ordering one party to pay out a ridiculous award in the absence of a contract. Marriage contracts should emulate the former. The time to work out the details of a marriage in demise is before entering into the marriage in the first place. As is practiced with golden parachutes by executives, who say, "Okay, I'll come run your company for so much salary, but in the event you get rid of me,

I want so much as my severance." No one holds a gun to the board of directors' heads and says, "Sign this." They have a choice; they could have said no. They didn't; they agreed.

This is exactly the scenario that should take place with marriage contracts. In the event of the breakdown of the marriage, the non-breadwinner should say, "I want this." It should be up to the breadwinner to agree or not.

Let's not stop there. The new and improved prenuptial should include all aspects of family law. It should not only cover property division, but it should also cover the matrimonial home, custody, child support, alimony, and any other clauses that the two parties wish to include. Years ago, the position was held by the courts that women were at a disadvantage when negotiating a prenuptial agreement. This certainly isn't the case anymore. Individual legal representation, and a specific time specification prior to the marriage, should be enough of a guarantee that both parties have not been prejudiced.

The courts should treat this new and improved contract just as they would any other contract in civil law. For either party to challenge the stipulations, the onus should be on the person challenging the contract, and not the other way around. They should have to prove without a shadow of a doubt that there is an excellent reason and justification for altering the contract. If some eighty-year-old billionaire agrees in a contract to leave his twenty-eight-year-old wife five hundred million upon his demise, or whatever is stipulated in the contract, then I'll be the first one to say, "Pay the woman what was agreed to." If a man agrees to pay his ex thirty thousand dollars a month for twenty years regardless if she cheats on him, steals from him, or for whatever reason, I would stand behind her right to be awarded the sum of the contract. Was it a dumb contract? Perhaps, but no one put a gun to his head and said, "Sign this." He did it voluntarily. This is how our Western civilization works in all areas of contracts and agreements. If business ran on the principles of family law, the economy would come to a grinding halt. But if someone wishes to limit the entitlement to her ex's opportunity cost when she entered the marriage, stipulate what the custody arrangements will be, set child support payments based on current costs of raising a child, and limit alimony to only what it would cost to get her back into the workforce, then this contract should be enforced as a valid agreement between two individuals who had independent legal advice and signed this of their own free will. This type of contract would indicate to both parties that no one is trying to take advantage of the other and no one has a hidden agenda in motives in entering this marriage. This would be the quintessential "no-fault" divorce settlement.

You won't find support from the divorce industry for this idea. The feminist movement would surely be outraged by such a change from the benefits they worked so hard to get in the seventies and eighties and have refined in the nineties.

To push this through, we have only one power. This is a tactic that works in all areas of social matters and in laws of business. Dupes in the Western world unite!

Abstain from marriage! We need to say, "No!" to marriage as we know it until the pendulum has swung back to its proper place. It won't swing back without a tremendous amount of effort, as there is a very strong force attempting to keep it exactly where it is. The thirty-billion-dollar divorce industry and the very well organized feminist movement will attempt to keep it exactly where it is.

Family Law Amendments

The following is addressed to all the men and women who are entrusted with creating the laws of the land in our Western world. I'm addressing this to the 550 individuals who represent us in Congress, the U.S. Senate, and the White House. That's really not such a big number of people required to reset a pendulum that has clearly swung too far and has such an important focus. This may very well be the tipping point to set us back on the track to appropriate work ethics, fairness, morals, and values.

What's at stake here is maintaining the institution of marriage. We are at risk of seeing the family unit, as we know it, vanish. To save this institution and the family, I propose the following:

1) *Custody.* This should be within federal jurisdiction and not left to individual states, provinces, or territories to vary or modify. All custody shall be joint or shared parenting unless there is a criminal reason to prevent it, or one parent waives their right to it. In the event that one parent leaves the jurisdiction

where the other parent resides, they would forfeit their custody as a result.

2) *Child Support.* Child support should be standard, regardless of income, and based on the costs of raising a child and not based on any other criteria. Only in the case of parties not able to pay this amount on a pro rata basis, a percentage of income should be imposed. All child support must be shared pro rata by the two parents.

3) *Alimony.* Unless otherwise stated, alimony should only be awarded as the minimum amount required to either enter the workforce, or re-enter the level of employment engaged in prior to the marriage. In the event that the universal amount received exceeds this minimum, then no alimony should be awarded.

4) *Marriage Contract.* It shall be mandatory to have a duly executed marriage contract, with independent legal advice, executed with enough time prior to a marriage. The contract must cover property division, and it may also cover custody, child support, alimony, and any other clause that the two independent parties wish to include in relation to their marriage. A marriage contract would be upheld like any other contract in our civil code. There should be a very low minimum for property division, and the onus should be on the non-breadwinner to demand entitlements through the marriage contract.

5) *Family Court.* Dissolve family court, as it won't be necessary. Contract disputes should be handled in civil

courts. Any allegations of child abuse or violence should be handled in criminal courts.

What's Next?

Power is not voluntarily withdrawn. It must be demanded by the victims of injustice. It will take an aggressive stance by some courageous legislators to take on the self-interests of a thirty-billion-dollar divorce industry in the U.S. alone. It will take a very strong and articulate legislator to stand up to the vocal and influential feminist movement, who will be adamant in maintaining their advantages.

I pose a scenario for you to ponder. If we dupes just said, "No! I refuse to enter into an unjust and one-sided agreement where one party (me) has everything to lose and one (her) has everything to gain," could you imagine what the demographics would look like a generation from now, if those who had the most at risk decided to abstain from marriage and forego creating a family? It would be a disaster. Our birth rate would go down, and the makeup of our demographics would change as those in a lower-income bracket continued to have families and the higher-income demographic abstained. As a result, we would have a lot fewer people to pay off our future debts, such as Social Security, government deficits, and Medicare.

This should be our argument as to why the pendulum must be reset. We have to vote by abstaining from marriage. What we demand is neither draconian nor repressive. Rather, we demand not to be put in a situation where we are susceptible to being duped, had, played, hoodwinked, bamboozled, tricked, conned, and exploited. No one is suggesting not looking after our responsibilities or putting anyone in a horrible situation. If marriage dissolution is to be truly "no fault," we can't have a system where one can profit from divorce.

I've written this book to inform the naïve and unknowing young men and, yes, women too, on the realities of our Gold Digger Nation and the laws and procedures that are currently in place. Just as one of the rites of passage is to communicate the "birds and the bees" to our children at a certain age, so too should you pass on the realities of our Gold Digger Laws to your sons, daughters, brothers, sisters, and even your mothers and fathers who are contemplating marriage. If nothing else, have your loved ones read this book or attend one of my lectures so they can receive the information for themselves and make an informed decision prior to entering the institution of marriage. You can also get more information at GoldDiggerNation.com, which outlines courses of action to reset the pendulum.

REFERENCES

Abraham, Jed, H. *From Courtship to Courtroom.* New York: Bloc Publishing Company, 1999.

Applewhite, Ashton. *Cutting Loose: Why Women Who End Their Marriages Do So Well.* New York: Harper Collins, 1997.

Baldwin, Alec. *A Promise to Ourselves.* New York: St. Martin's Press, 2008.

Baskerville, Stephen. *Taken Into Custody.* Nashville, TN: Cumberland House Publishing, 2007.

Cosby, Bill. *Fatherhood.* New York: Berkley Books, 1986.

Donovan, Sherri. *Hit Him Where It Hurt$.* Avon, MA: Adams Media, 2007.

Farrell, Warren. *The Myth of Male Power.* New York: Simon & Shuster, 1993.

Gladwell, Malcolm. *The Tipping Point.* New York: Little, Brown and Company, 2002.

Kruk, Edward. "Shared Parenting Responsibility: A Harm Reduction Based Approach to Divorce Law Reform." *Journal of Divorce and Remarriage* 43 (2005): 119–140.

Leving, Jeffery M. *Divorce Wars.* New York: Harper Collins, 2007.

Leving, Jeffery M., and Kenneth A. Dachman. *Fathers' Rights.* New York: Basic Books, 1997.

Parejko, Judy. *Stolen Vows: The Illusion of No-Fault Divorce and the Rise of the American Divorce Industry.* Collierville, TN: Instant Publisher, 2002.

Sawyer, Jerry. *Liberalism and the Age of the Woman.* Oakland, OR: Elderberry Press, 2006.

Sheppard, Roy, and Mary T. Cleary. *Venus: The Dark Side.* Somerset, England: Centre Publishing, 2008.

Simons, Frank. *Courts from Hell: Family Injustice in Canada.* Lulu.com, 2008.

Sommers, Christina Hoff. *Who Stole Feminism?: How Women Have Betrayed Women.* New York: Simon & Shuster, 1994.

Squire, Susan. *I Don't: A Contrarian History of Marriage.* New York: Bloomsbury, 2008.

Whelan, Christine, B. *Why Smart Men Marry Smart Women.* New York: Simon & Shuster, 2006.

ABOUT THE AUTHOR

Hal Roback is a two time victim of our family courts. He started with the intention of writing a very long letter to both his son and daughter about the ramifications of marriage in our Gold Digger Nation. This letter morphed into this book for his children, yours, and everyone contemplating marriage. Hal is a professional restaurateur, and owns a restaurant company. He is a graduate of a culinary school in New York, and holds a bachelor of science degree from Cornell University. All profits from this book and its associated products, will go to various causes committed to moving the pendulum back to the middle and making it safe to get married if one so chooses. He is a father of two, a son and a daughter, and is not married.